Master Numerology

By Robert Gandrup

ISBN-13: 978-0988922907
ISBN-10: 0988922908

1st Edition 2013

CONTENTS

INTRODUCTION

The Genius in Your Numbers

Michael Jackson and Albert Einstein were geniuses in their own fields. Both men had similar influences in their birth dates. Einstein's birth date also showed he was born to fulfill a higher purpose in life. Wouldn't it be great to have an operator's handbook to identify the genius in *your* life?

There's a better way to deal with life's challenges than trial and error. The ancient science of numerology is your handbook and it has what you need. It shows your hidden opportunities, how you make choices and what you can learn.

When you look at the birth information for famous people, there are a lot of similarities. These aren't just coincidences. Here's a quick look at more examples covered in this book.

George Washington and Thomas Jefferson had influences in their names that showed they were able to do things that few people could. Jefferson also had one in his birth date total. In his day, there were two calendars recognized. One was the old style that wasn't corrected for leap years and the new style that was. Either way showed he had a special mission in life. These men were born to fulfill a higher purpose and their lives definitely confirmed this.

Gandhi was often referred to as 'Mahatma' Gandhi. That wasn't his birth name but it meant he could be a very special kind of leader. His birthday showed he was born to be a pioneer and guide others to ultimate completion. He spent his life that way and was loved by millions.

Samuel Langhorne Clemens wrote under the pen name, Mark Twain. Both his birth name and pen name had the same influence that showed creative genius. No variation of his birth name would do the same. He chose exactly the best name for his needs.

Sergey Brin and Larry Page, co-founders of Google.com, both have identical influences in their birth dates that show they can do anything they set their minds to. Brin's name shows that he is a dynamic leader in business and Page's shows practical creativity in business. Each on his own could do almost anything. Together, the two of them are an unstoppable force. It would appear they were brought together for a combined higher purpose in life.

These are just a few examples of people who took advantage of the hidden forces at work in their lives. These and others will be covered in more detail further in this book.

Numerology reveals what you came here to do and how you can go about it. *Master Numerology* is written to show how you can know and use your natural strengths.

The Adventure Begins

In my teens, I met a well-known numerologist named Louise Snyfeld. My parents had gone to her and felt it would be good for me to do the same. They were right.

Louise followed the Eastern school of numerology. That approach is based on reincarnation and spiritual growth. It tells what to expect from life and how to go about it. Louise passed on a few years after we met but she changed my life in ways I wouldn't know for years to come.

Sometimes, I would feel on course. Other times it would seem that some key element was missing. I wanted answers. I read lots of books on numerology and studied how Louise did her calculations. It was fascinating and there always seemed to be more to know.

One day while fiddling with calculation methods, my attention was drawn to a number in my birth date I'd never seen defined. One calculation would show it and another wouldn't. Sometimes, I saw similar ones in other people's names or birth dates.

11, 22 and 33 are called *master numbers* and don't always get reduced to a lower value. What I noticed were higher master numbers from 44 to 99. Numerologists usually just reduce them to a lower value. It seemed to me that rules are rules and they had to be meaningful. Eagerly, I decided to see what they meant.

Information on 11 and 22 is plentiful. Every list of definitions has them. The meaning of 33 was not as common but still to be found. It was as though the higher ones just didn't exist. Determined to know more, I turned inward for guidance.

Initially, the task almost seemed impossible. But I don't believe in "impossible." If someone had done the lower ones, someone could do the rest. I could wait for "someone" to get the job done or do it myself. I wanted them right away so it was up to me. It never occurred to me that I might not be able to do it. Besides, I've heard it said that in a universe of all possibilities, everything exists. The information was there. All I had to do was go get it.

In some ways, the higher master numbers were easier to define than I expected. I looked at how 11, 22 and 33 were derived. Then I did the same with the "new" numbers. There were moments of inspiration and times of logical deduction. As I worked, they took shape.

Armed with the new definitions, I took another look at my name and birth date. Suddenly my whole life made sense. It was finally possible to see exactly what influences there were and what my focus should be. Previously unseen opportunities showed. Where life had seemed difficult, it now held meaning.

Excited, I checked names and birth dates for people I knew to see if the same was true for them. Where higher master numbers existed, it was. New insights were now possible.

This is the first book in a series that will show you how to get the most out of life. Master Numerology will guide you through the basics of numerology. Included in it are the definitions for all the master numbers from 11 through 99 and the triple numbers 000 through 999. Many of the ideas and calculations are my own. People who know something about numerology will be able to read through and pick out what they can use. For those who are new to it, this should get you going in the right direction.

PART ONE

The Basics

Things You Need to Know

This section gives you some necessary information to know what you're doing. Among other things, it shows how to calculate and read your influences. If you've done numerology before, you're already familiar with some of it. Go ahead and read it anyway. You may pick up something new. If nothing else, you'll have an idea of how it's done in this book. Best of all, there's no test at the end of the chapter. No one likes those things.

What is Numerology?

Numerology is the science of life. It's based on reincarnation and spiritual growth. Math is the language you use for that science. Before birth, you chose what to learn and how to go about it. Not every little detail but the basic outline, subject to your decisions and actions along the way. Numerology shows your potential and challenges. It tells how to make the best of situations and relationships. With the insight it gives, you can have a more fulfilling life.

In numerology, all calculations are done with numbers. Names, words and dates are given numeric values to work with. 0 (zero) really isn't a number but it has an influence.

Reduced Numbers

To reduce numbers to their basic single-digit value, add the digits within a number together. If that total is greater than 9, then do it again. For instance, 9790 is reduced like this:

9+7+9+0=25 and 2+5=7

The reduced value for 9790 is 7. It would be written this way:

3+7+9+0=25=7.

Driving Force

When you tell someone what make of car you have, you also say the year and model to be more specific. In addition to the basic influence of a reduced number, there is a way to tell more about what it means to you. That is the *driving force*.

You just saw 9790 reduced like this:

9+7+9+0=25=7

The main influence is 7, which is derived from 25. The 2 and 5 make the driving force. The driving force is the total digits before they're reduced.

883329718 totals to 49. It reduces to 13 then to 4. The driving force is 49. More insight is often possible when there is a number that reduces twice, as in the case with 49=13=4. Remember to use your intuition when you read these influences. If you have a strong feeling about how to interpret, it's most likely correct.

Master Numbers

When single digits are doubled up, they're called *master numbers*. A master number has an additional value to consider. It's similar to the driving force but with a more spiritual meaning. The single digit reduced number is the basic influence. The higher purpose indicated by the master number is built on that. In most instances, you consider both the master and reduced numbers. 11 would be written 11/2, 22 would be written 22/4 and so on. Add 21, 32 and 24 the total is 77. 21+32+24=77. You'd keep the 77 and reduce again to see what the lower value is. 7+7=14=5 so it would be written 77/5.

If you miss a master number, important opportunities could get overlooked. It's like driving a car with a 5-speed transmission using only 1st through 4th gears. You'd miss the full potential.

Triple Numbers

My wife and I headed out to buy an iPad. It would make her business more efficient and save time. Since time equals money, the purchase should make her income greater for each hour she spent. On the way out the door, I happened to glance at the clock. It said 1:11. Because of the inherent message, I knew this would mark a new phase in her professional life.

Triple numbers, numbers with all three digits the same, have special meaning. Occasionally, one will show up repeatedly. You look at the clock and it could be 5:55, 2:22 or something similar. The same triple number can catch your eye in other places, too. It could be a bus number, an address, part of a newspaper headline or literally anywhere. It's usually a message about something you should watch for or be aware of.

Triple numbers aren't often considered by most people. They can be a significant factor, though. They show opportunities and challenges, just like other numbers. When they appear, you should treat them much the same as you would a master number.

Multiples Add Meaning

When the year changed from 1999 to 2000, a major shift occurred. The basic way things work took a new direction and the World evolved.

1999 was the end of a thousand-year cycle. 1+999 meant the era of the individual leader was complete. We moved out of the time when a single person or force would rule supreme. The three 9s showed it was time for the world to look back and assess what had passed. There would be a new working model.

The year 2000 was the start of a new influence. The three 0s mean infinite potential of the 2. Cooperation is now the main influence for the next thousand years. Agreements and combined efforts get the best results. The years to come will define how the potential of 2 can be realized.

Numeric Values of Letters

Calculations in numerology are done with numbers. Dates are easy, the month can be written as a number. The day and year already are. It's slightly more involved with names or words. You first have to determine the numerical value of the letters. To do this, use the following table.

1	2	3	4	5	6	7	8	9
A	B	C	D	E	F	G	H	I
J	K	L	M	N	O	P	Q	R
S	T	U	V	W	X	Y	Z	

The letters under each number have that value. For example, H, Q and Z are under the number 8. The value for each of those is 8. For a word or name, look up the letter values and add them together. The numeric values in the name "John" are J=1, O=6, H=8, and N=5. The total for the name is 1+6+8+5=20=2. The vowels and consonants can be totaled separately to give additional meaning. That will be covered in the section on names. Occasionally, K is counted as 11, since it is the 11th letter in the alphabet and V as 22 since it is the 22nd. The table above shows the single digit values.

Signs

There are three *signs* in numerology. They are water, fire and air. Over the course of many lives, you progress through the water sign then the fire sign before finally entering the air sign. Once you're in the air sign, it's possible to grow beyond the need to incarnate. There are many ways to do it but most go back through the three signs again to prove what's been learned. Although it can be done in one lifetime, few do.

Each sign rules certain numbers. The signs and associated numbers are shown here.

Water – 1, 5, 7

Fire – 2, 4, 8

Air – 3, 6, 9

Your sign is shown by the day of the month you were born. For January 27, 1971, the day is 27. That reduces to 9 (2+7=9). A person with this birthday is in the air sign.

Daily Influence

Each day has a particular vibration. It's the sum of all the numbers in the date. 6/15/1900 would calculate this way:

6+1+5+1+9+0+0=22=4

The daily vibration is a 4. It can be called a '4 day.' Master numbers aren't used in this. Daily influences repeat every 9 days except when the month changes.

Prosperity Number

Each sign has a number that vibrates to success and prosperity. For the water sign, it is the number 5. For the fire sign, it is 8. For the air sign it's 6. Someone born on May 21, 1988 would be in the air sign. That makes the prosperity number 6.

Symphony Number

Music is vibration. Numbered pieces of music resonate to the numbers. A 1st symphony has the same energy as a 1 influence, a 2nd the same as a 2 and so on. Truly great composers feel universal vibrations and their music reflects that. Your *symphony number* is the same as your spiritual birthday. If yours is 5, you have a 5 symphony number. That symphony's energy is the same as your own. Relax on your spiritual birthday, put on the suitable symphony and enjoy.

Spiritual Birthdays

Your *spiritual birthday* is your birth date reduced to a single digit. Any days with the same influence are your spiritual birthdays. Your connection to the universal source is strongest on those days. It's easier to manifest what you want then.

Witness

Visualization is a powerful tool. When you state what you want in the presence of another person, you get great results. The other person witnesses what you want. Your statement of intent is a binding one between you and the higher powers. Anyone can be a witness. That person doesn't assume any responsibility or karma. This is a very effective way to get what you need.

On your spiritual birthday, it is easier to manifest what you want. Your connection to the universe is greater on those days than at any other time. Whatever you ask for will be yours. It may not happen immediately but it will come to you at the most appropriate time and in the most appropriate way. It doesn't hurt to have someone witness for you every time you have a spiritual birthday. Make sure you really want what you say. When it's yours, all the responsibility is too. If you do something that hurts someone or something, you reap the same yourself. If you don't feel comfortable enough to say your intent with a witness, you most likely know it isn't the right thing anyway.

State your need or intention in the positive tense. If you say something like, "I want to be rid of all my problems with my mother-in-law," you can really create problems for yourself. Your subconscious hears "problems with my mother-in-law" and brings more of them. Determine exactly what you want rather than what you don't want. Your subconscious only hears what you feel strongly about, not whether you want it or not. You can't push anything away but you can attract a replacement. It's better to say, "My relationship with my mother-in-law is more enjoyable and rewarding every day." Attraction is a universal rule and everything responds the same way. If this is the only thing you get from this book, you already have your value.

Here's the way it was taught by Louise Snyfeld:

Say to your witness,	"Today is my spiritual birthday, will you be my witness?"
Your witness should say,	"Yes, I will be your witness."
Say, "Today on my spiritual birthday, I ask that…" **State what it is you will manifest into your life.**	
Then say to your witness,	"You are my witness, I have said it."
Your witness should say,	"I am your witness, you have said it, so be it."

PART TWO

The Numbers

What the Numbers Are All About

Numbers have characteristics that can be seen at work in the physical world. When you move to a new address, change your name or make a major purchase, things change. You accept the differences and continue on without much thought. Think what it would be like if you could actually know those changes in advance. How would you react? Would you make the same move? With numerology, it's all very predictable. You know exactly what to expect BEFORE you move into that new home, buy that car or use a different name. You can plan your life and decide what changes you want to have. There is more about this in following chapters. You do need to know what the numbers mean, though. This section is about that.

The number and master number definitions have several parts. There is a descriptive comment at the top. After that, there is a general idea of what the number means. Next is *The Opportunity* with associated keywords. Keywords are good for a quick look and the text is a summation of how to get the most out of the influence. Lastly, there is *The Challenge* with keywords. That's how the number influence can express itself if you don't follow the opportunity in your life. Most people are a blend of opportunity and challenge. In fact, the challenge can alert you to some way to improve what you do in life. Very few live purely in the opportunity and the same is true for the challenge. Other numbers in your life affect what the number means, as well. At the end, there is a 'farmer' analogy for another perspective.

These are basic definitions of the numbers. There are more specific definitions in other sections of this book. They are all similar but have different perspectives. For example, a quality of the number 1 is self-sufficiency. That may mean you can take care of yourself. It could also mean you need to develop that quality. As a challenge, it might be that you have obstacles to your ability to stand on your own two feet or you are too independent and ignore help when it's needed.

The number definitions tell you what each number means BY ITSELF. You also have to consider what other numbers there are in your life. It's much like playing a guitar. Each string has a sound. Pluck several of them together and you have a chord that sounds entirely different.

In the following definitions, there are three categories of numbers. First are the primary numbers 1 through 9. They show the essential vibrations of the numbers. For lack of a better place to put it, 0 (zero) is also included in this set of numbers.

After that come the master numbers. These are double digit numbers with both digits the same. It includes 11, 22 and others up to 99. The master numbers show the higher values of numbers.

Lastly there are the triple numbers. These are three-digit numbers where all three are the same like 111, 222 and so on. In addition to opportunities and challenges, they also can give you special messages to help you along.

Get familiar with the numbers. When you understand them, you're well on your way.

PRIMARY Numbers – Essential Vibrations

0
—————————————————————— **Potential**

Zero is everything or nothing. It amplifies whatever it stands next to as pure potential.

Zero (0) is the most powerful number. Like a diamond, it has no particular color but all colors are in it at the purest level. It's the starting point where things can go in any direction. It can be nothing, a way of holding space without content. It can also be pure potential ready to turn into something identifiable.

The Opportunity

Transmutation	Growth	Nothing
All possibilities	Perfection	Everything
Pure Potential	Extremes	Continuous
Infinite	Intense	Powerful
Formless	Chaos	Amplify
Limitless	Void	Wild Card
Universal	Rebirth	

0 is infinite potential waiting to be given form. It represents the cycle of birth, death and rebirth. 0 is complete and infinitely available. By itself, it means all or nothing. It stands for great transformation and growth. It can bring extremes or greatly amplify any quality. When it follows another number, it boosts

tne potential of that number. It can mean that all the qualities of the root number are available to the fullest degree.

The Challenge

Unfulfilled	Confusion	Sarcastic
Limitation	Discomfort	Hateful
Difficulty	Imbalance	Cruel
Burden	Irritable	Criminal
Aimlessness	Spiteful	Violence
Unpredictable	Disagreeable	

Without direction, the energy of 0 can be lost or overlooked. The potential may be unrealized, misunderstood or misused. If that happens, it becomes just empty space with no form, direction or benefit. When the opportunity is missed, it can lead to lashing out in any number of ways. A person could get dissatisfied with life. That could cause one to be mad at the world and blame others for lack or failure. In that case, life could seem like a waste. The longer the potential stagnates, the worse it gets.

The farmer sees great potential in the empty field. He can make it be anything he wants.

1

_____ **Conception**

Like all pioneers, 1 goes into the unknown and sets the direction for others to follow.

1 is the beginning of a cycle. It is creation, instigation and a fresh start. After 0, 1 is the next strongest number. This is the time to prepare for the future and start new things. Activities & ventures begun under a 1 influence have the best chance of success. When the 1 follows a 9, the seeds of the coming cycle have their origins in the end of the previous one and build on what's been accomplished.

The Opportunity
Self-motivation	Start	Progressive
Independent	Creation	Individuality
Determination	Innovative	Courage
Self-sufficient	Instigation	Confidence
Beginning	Leadership	Ambition
Pioneer	Initiative	Focus
New	Originality	

1's are self-reliant and ambitious. They make good leaders. They're pioneers, willing to step into the unknown to see what's there and make something from it. They branch out from normal lines of thought and lay the groundwork for others to follow. They offer original ideas and exciting, new solutions. Their confidence, ambition and leadership qualities help them carry out ideas in the pursuit of dreams. A 1 influence is the best to start something new. It's the perfect time to have a wedding, begin projects, make important appointments, start a new job, meet new people, or make a major change in your life. New ideas mature easily.

The Challenge

Ineffective	Indecision	Bullying
Dependent	Apathy	Narcissism
Insecure	Stubborn	Repressive
Careless	Egotistical	Vindictive
Resentful	Self-serving	Criminal
Defensive	Aggression	
Procrastination	Domination	

If not properly disciplined, these strong people can go to extremes. One extreme means unbridled self-interest and a lack of regard for others. They could feel that any means to a goal is acceptable. At the other extreme, they can be totally ineffective. This could mean time and effort is wasted with no results to show for it. A genuine concern for others is necessary to reach the full potential of the 1 influence.

The farmer prepares the soil and plants seeds for the new crop.

2 ————————————————— **Cooperation**

The real power of 2 is to combine efforts with another so the result is greater than either can accomplish alone.

The second part of a cycle is 2. It's partnering of all kinds, harmony, diplomacy and service. Partnerships and work groups thrive. 2 means cooperation with others, especially in a supportive role. Well thought-out plans and combined ideas get good results.

The Opportunity

Encouragement	Modest	Support
Responsible	Cooperation	Planning
Partnership	Caring	Assistance
Marriage	Mediation	Balance
Sharing	Harmony	Rhythm
Commitment	Diplomacy	Symmetry
Alliance	Sensitivity	Subtlety
Interaction	Tact	Patience
Loving	Service	

The real strength for 2s is relationships. That can be with themselves, other people, situations, things or ideas. Comfort comes from love, marriage and partnerships. They have a natural ability to get along with others. They like to share their experiences and interests with others. They enjoy harmony in all forms from music and nature to well-functioning groups. 2s do best when allowed to quietly work things out. People with this as a main influence are attracted to strong-willed people for direction and opportunity. They're great at consolation and encouragement. Subtlety and quiet suggestions get results for them. Quite often, they are the force behind the throne. They achieve personal goals when they propel others to success.

The Challenge

Hyper-sensitive	Fearful	Rude
Uncooperative	Easily swayed	Devious
Dependent	Insecure	Manipulative
Shy	Careless	Paranoid
Indecisive	Discontented	Schizophrenic
Needy	Resentful	
Finicky	Pessimistic	

Without proper direction, the opportunity turns inward. 2s could either withdraw or get aggressive. Withdrawn, they may try to hide from what they don't understand. Lashing out can be a fear reflex for them. When aggressive, they may try to control others. Extreme cases can be very unbalanced. Without a genuine concern for others, those with this influence could become dishonest or cruel.

The farmer waters and works with the land so the seeds will germinate and start to grow.

3
_____ **Creativity**

Self-expression is the force that moves a 3 to expose his or her inner being for all to see.

Ideas and events move forward with flair. Creativity and self-expression make 3 the life blood of an artist. New ideas are brought forth from universal sources. One's inner feelings are expressed in the world. It can be visual, verbal or any other kind of communication.

The Opportunity

Creativity	Innovation	Friendly
Self-expression	Ideas	Popular
Communication	Originality	Kind
Entertainment	Imagination	Emotional
Sociable	Intelligence	Enthusiasm
Artistic	Skill	Optimism
Clever	Dexterity	Happy

This is pure creativity. It's what is expressed by an artist, writer or entertainer. It means good dexterity and the ability to work skillfully. 3s can do just about anything with their hands. They can work with tiny watch parts or huge hunks of steel. They're good communicators and get their point across when they want to. They like social interaction and can be very entertaining. Intelligent and clever, they have lots of interesting ideas to offer. They're always welcome at gatherings. An audience really brings out the best in them. Their joviality may affect those around them and the way they laugh can be contagious. They show imagination and originality in everything they do. At times, they can be very emotional. Their intuition is strong. Often, they show pure genius in their field of endeavor. They can turn almost anything into a thing of beauty.

The Challenge

Confused	Antisocial	Superficial
Insecurity	Trivial	Incoherent
Unfocused	Opinionated	Uninformative
Bragging	Boring	Unethical
Illogical	Wasteful	Deceitful
Whining	Impatient	Destructive
Eccentric	Gossiping	

If creativity isn't expressed, 3s might feel blocked in life. They may not even realize this when it happens. The need to communicate can lead to incessant talking or complete withdrawal. Creative people who don't consider the needs of others could get self-absorbed. Communication and creativity without direction may cause compulsive lying. In worse cases, they can be destructive. Self-control and a practical approach are needed to get the most from this influence.

The farmer is joyous. His field, once bare dirt, now thrives with new life as seeds sprout and shoots break ground.

4

—————————————————————— **Practicality**

In the case of 4, the true reward is found in the project itself and how it is carried out.

Application and diligence get the job done. 4 means to do what is needed, when it's needed. Dependability and patriotism are key traits. Progress may seem slow but a solid foundation produces results later on. Have patience and pay attention to detail. Keep your nose to the grindstone, it's time to take care of business.

The Opportunity

Concentration	Dependable	Capable
Organization	Loyal	Results
Application	Responsible	Economical
Work	Patriotic	Disciplined
Diligence	Conservative	Cautious
Practicality	Honesty	Trustworthy
Details	Devotion	Logical
Orderly	Duty	
Patience	Dexterity	

4s get results by hard work and an orderly approach. People with this influence are trustworthy, practical and capable. They do well in positions that require concentration and diligence. For them, logic is preferable to emotions and impulsiveness. They like to be busy. For them, the work itself is a greater reward than its results. When a job requires a steady, organized approach, they're the ones to have on the job. They can be the backbone of a business or project. When 4 is one's destiny number, it can give a measure of relief from the difficulty that often seems to come with this influence.

The Challenge

Workaholic	Dull	Vulgar
Overworked	Slow	Jealous
Tunnel vision	Dogmatic	Rude
Disorganized	Inefficient	Vindictive
Illogical	Incompetent	Cruel
Headstrong	Lazy	Inhuman
Nit-picky	Failure	
Narrow-minded	Destructive	

If 4s don't do something fulfilling, work can become a chore. It's important for them to apply their abilities productively to see rewards. Without that, they could blame others for their own failures or shortcomings. Too much attention to details can make them overlook the overall scope of a task. If not focused properly, they can feel overworked. At the worst, they can become violently inhuman. It's important for 4s to focus on the end result and work toward that.

The shoots grow into healthy plants. The farmer works hard to weed, water, stake plants and control pests.

5
_____ **Freedom**

Always an adventure, 5 is alive with variety, transformation and excitement.

5 is freedom of thought, word and action. This is to enjoy new and exciting things in life. It is also positive change. What's old transforms into something new. One must be adaptable and ready to make choices. It can mean public events, socializing and travel. Previous work now starts to show results as things start to take a new form.

The Opportunity

Change	Excitement	Variety
Transformation	Freedom	Sensuality
Communication	Versatile	Amiable
Enthusiasm	Adaptable	Courage
Progress	Clever	Risk
Active	Friendly	Social
Travel	Intelligent	Attractive
Adventure	Quick	Salesman

5s meet the world on their own terms and come out ahead. They like to experience life in all its splendor. They're full of limitless energy and have many interests. They look youthful and attractive. They can fly across cross the country, attend an important event, return, climb off the plane, go out for a night on the town and never run down or look tired. They love the

company of friends and acquaintances, particularly of the
opposite sex. Clever and witty, they have something to add to
any conversation. They can talk with anyone on their own level.
5s seem to make the best of any situation and adjust to new
conditions quickly. They can be good writers or actors. Travel
suits them and borders don't make any difference. Their minds
and movements are quick. They can handle people without
anyone ever suspecting it.

The Challenge

Boredom	Superficial	Manipulative
Inconsistency	Flighty	Perversion
Irresponsible	Trite	Addiction
Undependable	Impulsive	Abuse
Reckless	Careless	Hyper sexuality
Inconsiderate	Self-indulgent	Depravity
Disorganized	Thoughtless	

People with this as a main influence may be irresponsible or
undependable. The love of fast action can make 5s careless.
They can get bored easily and might not stay focused on the job
at hand. The love of physical sensations can turn to addiction.
They may not think things through before acting. In extreme
cases 5s can show depravity or be destructive. The 5 energy
must be channeled properly. A practical approach can balance
them and bring them down to Earth.

The farmer is excited to see the plants mature and take
new form. They first produce buds, then blossoms.

6

Nurturing

6 is all the energy of a patriarch to be used where one takes care of a family or other group.

The head of a family brings harmony and balance to disputes. 6 is all the qualities of home and family. "Family" can be a spouse, children, neighbors, friends, co-workers, community, the country or the world. It's loving care as one extends to family members. It includes a strong sense of service, nurturing and fairness.

The Opportunity

Responsible	Kind	Solutions
Understanding	Dutiful	Harmony
Communication	Sympathy	Stability
Selflessness	Empathy	Fairness
Home	Love	Ideals
Family	Idealism	Mediator
Community	Devotion	Advisor
Domestic	Nurturing	Balance
Service	Protective	Guidance

6's have strong protective instincts. They are good parents or care-givers. They have an acute sense of right and wrong. Marriage or community involvement is where they really do well. They bring harmony from a place of love and understanding. Great mediators, they find fair solutions and promote open discussion between opposing parties. Others open up easily to a 6 and will listen to new ideas from them. People with this as a main influence are confident and comfortable with others. They do well in service-oriented professions. They're great as the head of a family and make good advisors to corporate heads or world leaders. Mission statements are a good use of this influence.

The Challenge

Controlling	Worry	Nosy
Intolerant	Cynicism	Smug
Manipulative	Egotism	Discontented
Interfering	Suspicious	Tyrannical
Meddlesome	Jealousy	Dictatorial
Dominating	Selfishness	
Anxiety	Burdensome	

Without concern for the needs of others, 6s may become self-absorbed. They could try to manipulate people to get what they want. 6 people can feel that they are absolutely right in any situation. In their opinion, anyone opposed is wrong. They have to understand that others have different viewpoints and needs. They must also learn that there are times when it's necessary to let others work things out on their own.

The farmer cares for the young fruit so it can grow and develop. He feels connected to his land and crops.

7

———————————————————————— **Ripening**

A 7 is self-sufficient and methodically finds the best answers to complex questions.

A person who works alone can come up with his own answers. For a 7, wisdom and guidance comes from within. It's the confident use of one's own resources. This means to gather and analyze information without help from others. Meditation and occult studies can be a large part of the process.

The Opportunity

Preparedness	Occult	Intuition
Perseverance	Study	Perfection
Spirituality	Research	Confidence
Wisdom	Analysis	Self-reliance
Guidance	Investigation	Individuality
Introspection	Information	Methodical
Faith	Meditation	Thorough

7's like to be thorough. These people do well in analytical fields like psychology or science. As investigators, they're naturals. They like to meditate and quietly process information to get solutions. Interruptions or outside help aren't welcomed. Not much for teamwork, 7's are independent. They're confident and come up with perfect solutions on their own. They're innovative in how they deal with problems but need time to go over the possibilities. They have inner peace and a natural dignity. Others may think they're loners but that's fine with them. Their strength is to be satisfied with the results they get. Only after they have solved a problem, will they share that with others. They usually get the last word in. They may develop an interest in spirituality, religion or the occult.

The Challenge

Withdrawn	Fussy	Pessimism
Antisocial	Cynical	Materialism
Self-centered	Sarcastic	Addiction
Inconsiderate	Skeptical	Theft
Aloof	Nervous	Intolerance
Indifferent	Secretive	Deceit
Unreceptive	Careless	Paranoia
Isolationist	Frustrated	
Melancholy	Depressed	

Without direction, 7s may show poor judgment. They could withdraw completely from people and social contact. Close friends may not be possible. They may not welcome necessary help from others. Self-absorption can make them inconsiderate of other people's feelings. In a relationship, they could be unfaithful. 7s should learn to understand others and their needs.

The farmer watches the crops ripen. He takes inventory of what he will need when the harvest time comes and prepares for the busy time ahead.

8

Harvest

All the rewards of past labors are now enjoyed under an 8 influence.

Previous efforts now show results. Success is usually associated with finances but it can be a lot more than that. It's to be found in any activity where you work to get a result. This comes from organization and the wise use of one's time.

The Opportunity

Achievement	Tasteful	Finances
Dependability	Polite	Money
Success	Triumph	Organization
Strength	Diplomacy	Practicality
Prosperity	Management	Power
Efficiency	Application	Networking
Aggressive	Goals	Internet
Intelligent	Plans	
Sensible	Business	

Profit is the result of effort spent. 8s make good managers. Authority and power suit them well. They are practical and know how to get people to do their best. The business world is their playground. They're at home with financial plans, accounting systems or production schedules. They make powerful friends and allies in strategic positions. They're not limited to just money matters, though. Their abilities are useful in all areas of life and 8s do well in any activity that needs diplomacy or organization. Their good judgment comes from levelheadedness and determination. Networking is as natural as breathing for them. They are most successful when they consider the needs of those who work with them on a project.

The Challenge

Greed	Materialistic	Unscrupulous
Loss	Domineering	Lethargic
Failure	Self-centered	Superficial
Low Self-esteem	Inconsiderate	Cruel
Grasping	Intolerant	Dishonest
Needy	Power-hungry	Criminal
Powerless	Callous	

People reap what they sow. If that is negative or out of balance, the harvest will be in keeping. When nothing has been invested, there is no reward. Low self-esteem can result. Those with this challenge can be very negative and blame others for problems. Extreme cases could be criminally self-serving or murderous. Tolerance and fairness is needed. Concern for the needs of others helps to insure success.

Crops are ripe and the farmer is busy with the harvest. He happily picks the produce and takes it to the market. All his past efforts now pay off.

9 ——————————————— Completion

Like a maestro, 9 puts all the elements of the other numbers together in balance.

9 is complete and contains some of all the other numbers. It is time to take care of unfinished business and reflect on all that has happened to now. One both prepares for the future and confirms what's been learned. 9 is also strength and balance in leadership.

The Opportunity

Retrospection	Creativity	Appreciation
Understanding	Trustworthy	Compassion
Universality	Fairness	Service
Completion	Intuition	Tolerant
Balance	Philanthropy	Benevolent
Honesty	Strength	Assessment
Ethics	Optimism	
Idealism	Leadership	

Strong with drive and energy, 9's are in charge. They make good humanitarians and leaders. They know what they want and are capable of great achievements. They understand people and like to share with them. 9's are magnetic, efficient and honest. They have a strong artistic sense and can add a personal flair to any activity. Romantics by nature, they may tend to be emotional at times. They are sympathetic to others and sensitive to their needs. They do well in positions that can benefit others. They make good judges because of their understanding and fairness. Fulfillment is theirs through ethics and high ideals.

The Challenge

Unbalanced	Impractical	Self-centered
Egocentric	Blaming	Dishonest
Judgmental	Unfocused	Unethical
Condemning	Immoral	Deceitful
Base	Crude	Corrupt
Low Self-esteem	Cold	Criminal
Undependable	Stingy	
Over-emotional	Intolerant	

If power is abused, it can lead to a lack of support from key people. Dishonesty or lack of ethics can bring retribution to 9s. People may ignore what they have to say if they're too forceful, dramatic or adamant. There can be a tendency to disregard the needs of others. Those with this influence should strive for balance on all levels. It helps to work with others and consider their needs.

The farmer cleans up after the harvest. He puts equipment away and organizes for the next season. Looking back, he assesses past efforts and achievements. The next crop is grown from the seeds saved this season.

MASTER Numbers – Higher Values

11
——————————————————————————Creative Idealist

Idealists, visionaries and innovators are embodied in the master number 11.

A dreamer who's creative is called a visionary. The first master number is 11. It shows both innovation and vision. 11 is great new ideas for the betterment of all. It means leadership and idealism in the purest form. These qualities are found in inspirational teachers and spiritual leaders.

The Opportunity

Enlightenment	Service	Dreamer
Understanding	Selfless	Optimist
Communication	Fame	Magnetic
Illumination	Recognition	Visionary
Idealism	Publicity	Diplomacy
Awareness	Limelight	Insight
Love	Creative	Inspiration
Intuition	Sensitive	Leadership
Spirituality	Channeling	

11s do best when they serve mankind. They can see the divine in everything. They know why they're here and want to help others find their higher purpose. A strong sense of intuition can get them through difficult times. 11s are good communicators and enjoy personal interaction. People are intuitively attracted to them and they're a welcome addition to any gathering. They like the limelight and do well speaking in public. Highly creative, they enjoy art, music and beauty in all its forms. They can display genius in their chosen field. They often put the interests of others ahead of their own.

The Challenge

Impractical	Unfathomable	Mismanage
Frustrated	Overwhelmed	Incompetent
Confused	Miserly	Inefficient
Withdrawn	Dishonest	Depressed
Insecure	Devilish	Aloof
Fanatical	Shiftless	Closed-minded
Decadent	Devious	

11s can have grand ideas but may lack the practical skills to carry them to completion. Without a good plan of action, they can get overwhelmed, frustrated or insecure. 11s can get reclusive or spend too much time in pursuit of self-oriented goals. They excel when there are more practical people around to give direction. In service to others is how 11s work best but it's important to tend to their own needs as well.

The farmer sees how to help others make their fields more productive. He offers guidance and inspiration at meetings and gatherings. He's widely known for his ideas.

22 ——————————— Master Builder

The 22 is a practical idealist who can do anything he decides to undertake.

There is a bridge between the worldly and the divine. 22 can use that bridge. It can turn an idealistic vision into a reality. First, key elements must be identified. From that, an organized plan can be formulated. True success comes from the practical use of spiritual principles.

<u>The Opportunity</u>

Organization	Planning	Intuitive
Accomplish	Ambition	Ingenious
Philanthropic	Inspired	Generous
Practical	Vision	Capable
Idealistic	Wisdom	Analyze
Spirituality	Goals	Alternative
Leadership	Imaginative	Patterns
Honesty	Champion	Solutions
Builder	Diplomacy	Confidence

22s are goal-oriented and realistic. Gifted with vision, they can see the complete scope of a project in detail. They're organized and immensely capable. They find solutions where others see only chaos. They can do anything from simple projects to vast co-creative ones. When in charge of a project, they find the best way to get it done. If they work for others, they have useful suggestions that make the job more effective. They use spiritual values in every day projects and take practical ideas to a spiritual level. 22s are the creative geniuses of business. They excel when their work is for the greater good. They can be the champion of a cause, a gifted diplomat or a philanthropist.

The Challenge

Unsuccessful	Fearful	Vicious
Self-centered	Negative	Tyrannical
Detached	Small-minded	Manipulative
Impersonal	Scheming	Vindictive
Incapacitated	Greedy	Heartless
Incompetent	Dogmatic	Destructive
Unfocused	Unsuccessful	Hateful
Lazy	Spiteful	Violent

If not focused on service, 22s may encounter obstacles. Their expansive energy can turn inward and make them unable to accomplish much. They may blame others for their failings. Worse cases can be destructive or violent. It helps for them to find a way to help others reach their goals. They need a project to work on so they get a sense of accomplishment.

The farmer comes up with detailed, practical plans to make land more productive. He shows others how to be more successful.

33 —————————————— Spiritual Service

The loving strength of a 33 really shows when one becomes a healer of the body or spirit.

33 is the defender of the underdog who sets the scales in balance. Service to others is an important part of this influence. Its real power, though, is to help others grow on many levels. It's about self-realization and enlightenment. Those with this influence are often awakened to their own divine light.

The Opportunity

Understanding	Divine Love	Compassion
Enlightened	Nurturing	Selflessness
Empowerment	Spirituality	Wisdom
Master	Healer	Responsible
Spiritualist	Inspire	Dutiful
Master Teacher	Service	Stable
Spiritual	Harmony	Devoted
Guidance	Tolerance	Community
Spiritual Leader	Patience	Champion

33s are spiritualists that work on higher levels. They can heal others and give them new life. Those with this influence inspire others to do their best. They want to see everyone reach their highest potential. They're at home in the health care field, especially when associated with natural cures and herbalism. Many are faith healers or the best of doctors. In addition to physical health, they want to help people in other ways, too. They are fully aware there is no real difference between spiritual and worldly issues. The highest rewards for them are found in actions that benefit many.

The Challenge

Anxiety	Self-absorption	Interfering
Aggression	Self-centered	Manipulative
Self-doubt	Egotistical	Dishonest
Cynicism	Intolerant	Subversive
Distrust	Discontented	Tyrannical
Envy	Obstructive	

If self-centered, a 33 could try to demean the efforts or achievements of others. When self-confidence erodes, they can turn against any who disagree with them. They could see an effort to help as a threat rather than as a genuine offer of assistance. They might be suspicious of those who would help them reach a goal. At the worst, they can be violently aggressive. It's important for them to pursue activities that benefit people on a large scale. The larger the scale, the better.

The farmer shows other farmers how to correct soil deficiencies and improve their methods. His goal is to help them reach their own highest potential.

44 ——————————— Spiritual Application

Like a sage, 44 expresses spirituality in both divine and worldly activities to prove there is no difference between them.

Divine principles can be expressed in all parts of life. 44 is the use of spiritual principles in all worldly activities. It shows that higher values help in daily life. This influence favors projects that are for the benefit of all. It is to meet people's material needs, then teach them to provide for themselves in the future.

The Opportunity

Divine	Efficient	Aggressive
Awareness	Empowerment	Polite
Convergence	Intelligent	Tasteful
Focused	Patience	Conviction
Global Purpose	Realization	Balance
Practical	Wisdom	Application
Spirituality	Strength	Vision
Spiritual Values	Heroism	Planning
Good Judgment	Self-control	Discipline

44s are gifted with power and vision. They see the divine in everything. They want to make a vast difference in how the people of the world apply themselves. For them, the use of higher principles is the only way to get a job done right. This can be in business or their personal lives. They use insight, careful planning and vision to see a project through to completion. Rather than something they do, it's an integral part of life for them. They know the world is the physical expression of our inner selves. They don't just want to help people have what they need. They want people to be able to take care of themselves. They often work where they can make the worldly home of mankind better for future generations.

The Challenge

Poor judgment	Prejudice	Unethical
Imprudent	Delusional	Difficult
Lethargic	Egotistic	Power-hungry
Impatient	Greedy	Unscrupulous
Unaware	Heartless	Cruel
Obstructive	Inconsiderate	Self-serving
Dishonest	Materialistic	

Without higher values to guide them, 44s can be short-sighted. They may pursue purely material goals. It's possible they could ignore the needs of others for their own benefit. At the worst, they could be criminally self-serving. There may be considerable inner struggle if they don't try to help others. They do best to focus on what is right for large numbers of people.

The farmer helps other farmers see there's is more to agriculture than just profit. He shows them how to express the divine in their land and in the service they provide.

55

Universal Leader

As shown by 55, a great leader can successfully lead any kind of group regardless of the situation.

Gifted leadership combines with intuitive skills to help large numbers of people. Total freedom is the main attribute. The true pioneer spirit in them gets results where others may fail. It supports new concepts, avenues, places and ways of thinking. There's a real need to work for the greatest good of all.

The Opportunity

Master Guide	Natural Leader	Exuberance
Awareness	Self-sufficient	Intuition
Clarity	Freedom	Knowledge
Determination	Travel	Recognition
Integration	Pioneer	Clairvoyance
Cognizance	Wisdom	Telepathy
Born Traveler	Memory	Seeker
Prominence	Ambition	Oneness
Unified Thinking	Organization	

55s are great leaders. They're very capable and easily lead projects that help large numbers of people. They can take any size or type of group to greatness. Borders and normal boundaries don't matter to them at all. They can work anywhere on the planet or get dissimilar groups to work with each other. They're able to think on their feet and act quickly. They make great military commanders. With a true pioneer spirit, they will forge new paths for others to follow. 55s have a superb memory and tend to be clairvoyant. These people are especially interested in spirituality and metaphysics. They enjoy the excitement of life on all levels. Public recognition gives them a special boost.

The Challenge

Excessive	Inconsiderate	Oppression
Irritable	Procrastinating	Manipulation
Over-indulgent	Domineering	Perversion
Ironic	Bullying	Over-ambitious
Cynical	Interfering	Back-biting
Stubborn	Self-serving	Narcissism
Egotistical	Controlling	

If 55s don't work for the benefit of others, they can get self-centered and over-indulgent. They may be rude or inconsiderate. Their leadership qualities may be ignored and their self-esteem can erode. They might pursue their own goals at the expense of other people. Criminal actions may be part of that, too. It's important for them to find projects that help others. In doing so, they also reach their own goals.

The farmer travels great distances to help others make their farms more productive. He starts projects with new and innovative ideas. He's well known for his contributions.

66

_____ **Higher Purpose**

When disputes arise, the selfless mediator finds a solution that's acceptable to both.

A caring and just leader watches over those under him. He finds solutions to disputes that both sides agree on. It's all the qualities found in a loving parent. This is the perfect expression of family values. The 66 includes a spiritual approach, as well. World issues are particularly suited for one with this influence.

The Opportunity

Domestic	Devoted	Family
Awareness	Service	Responsible
Spiritual Leader	Optimism	Expressive
Communicative	Stable	Loyal
Peacemaker	Popular	Arbitrator
Universal Love	Sensible	Generous
Transmutation	Joyous	Kind
Negotiator	Affable	Moralist

66s are peacemakers. They want to make the place we live better for all people in every way possible. This is especially true with children and family. To them, "family" can be close relatives or it can be all of mankind. The universe is their home and they answer to the highest order. They can negotiate a peace treaty or settle a dispute between siblings. They work well for a global peace organization, in diplomatic service or as a public servant in the local community. They make great spiritual leaders. They're kind and liked by just about everyone. They know the true meaning of family ideals.

The Challenge

Withdrawn	Submissive	Judgmental
Uncooperative	Smug	Condemning
Boring	Difficult	Intrusive
Pontificating	Meddling	Rowdy
Over-emotional	Interfering	Egotistical
Manipulative	Gossiping	Unstable
Aggression	Deceitful	

66s that don't work for the greater good can be difficult. Instead of respect, they may earn disdain from those around them. That could cause them to get emotional or aggressive. It's possible they could have a dangerously narrow focus and pursue a project that helps a few at the great expense of others. Extreme cases may be unstable and unpredictable. The goal of the 66 must be the betterment of all, whether they are directly involved or not.

The farmer gets the farming community to agree on issues. He settles disputes and works out solutions to problems. People love him for the help he gives to all.

77
────────────────────────────── **Applied Wisdom**

With insight, pure intent and an inner connection to spirit, 77 brings situations into balance.

The main forces are awareness and creative genius. It's the use of universal forces to affect situations or events. This is very much about the power of the mind. The creative power of the universe gets focused to bring results. With pure intent, it can be used to help others.

The Opportunity

Spiritual	Wise Counsel	Prolific
Awakened	Pure Mind	Sensual
Loving	Intuition	Insight
Connected	Intelligent	Mysticism
Calm Judgment	Inventive	Wisdom
Applied Intention	Enthusiastic	Healer
Creative Genius	Charismatic	Shaman

77s are fully aware of their connection to the infinite. They're not too concerned with the issues of the world. Their abilities are mostly a result of their own research and meditation. They understand people in a way that is far beyond what most suspect possible. With loving detachment, they allow others to live and learn on their own. They usually offer guidance only when asked or if they see it's absolutely necessary. They're good at remote healing. They can achieve great public presence. They make good prophets, sages or spiritualists. Their talents are best used to help others on a higher level.

The Challenge

Self-absorption	Pontification	Unfocused
Manipulative	Aloof	Spiteful
Careless	Smug	Hateful
Trivial	Egotistic	Black Arts
Untrustworthy	Tyrannical	Vengeful
Incompetent	Bragging	Arrogant
Withdrawn	Impulsive	

77s could use their abilities for selfish means. They may ignore the physical world to study religion or the occult. They might try to manipulate others to suit their desires. As well, they could get over confident and take needless risks. In extreme cases, they may get involved with voodoo, black magic or Satanism. They must find constructive ways to use their unique abilities.

The farmer is a renowned agricultural consultant. He focuses his mind to create real solutions. Both the farmers and those who enjoy the crops benefit from his efforts.

88

Mastering Abundance

Spiritual principles are what make 88 the total master of the business world.

88 is the mastery of success and abundance. There can be balance between them. They can both support and include the other. Success is usually associated with the physical world and its values. 88 is the use of spiritual principles to achieve worldly ends. It proves that true success comes with selflessness.

The Opportunity

Master Disciple	Awareness	Achievement
Spiritual	Spirituality	Abundance
Integration	Selfless	Simplicity
Altruistic	Benevolent	Discipline
Natural Beauty	Mystic	Balance
Responsibility	Artistry	Prepared
Discrimination	Self-Control	Organized

Abundance is much more than just monetary wealth. It's to be found in all areas of life. 88's are self-motivated and self-disciplined. They apply spiritual values in everything they do. They can use power and control with discrimination. They're responsible and plan their actions with care. 88s overcome temptation to reach fair solutions. They do best when their work is for the benefit of many. Sometimes they seem to be made of contradictions but really they're the spiritual masters of the business world.

The Challenge

Aimless	Headstrong	Pessimistic
Ineffective	Aloof	Dogmatic
Unfocused	Cynical	Fanatical
Irresponsible	Superficial	Greedy
Insensitive	Fussy	Cruel
Untrustworthy	Uncaring	Dishonest
Indiscriminate	Insensitive	Materialistic
Disorganized	Tense	Domineering

Although 88s can have worldly success, they must consider the impact their actions have on others. They may get short-sighted or rigid in thought and action. They could be insensitive to other people's needs. At the worst, they can show sociopathic behavior. It's important to include others in their plans and goals. Some of their success-building energy needs to be devoted to home and family. Otherwise, there could be obstacles and failure for them.

The farmer has mastered all aspects of agriculture. He can make any farm highly productive. A true artist of the land, he builds a farming empire that benefits all.

99
Divine Wholeness

The completion, illumination and balance of 99 are seen in an enlightened being.

The completion of a cycle is the gateway to the next. It's the confirmation of previous lessons. At this point, one achieves enlightenment and wholeness on every level. It's time to apply what has been learned. The next step is to help others grow.

The Opportunity

Divine Fullness	Tolerance	Eternal
Artistic Genius	Awareness	Proving
Cosmic Love	Illumination	Healing
Enlightenment	Insight	Appreciation
Unity	Compassion	Honesty
Immortality	Selflessness	Ethics
Completion	Mentoring	Gateway
Evolution	Communion	Resurrection

99s experience life completely. They show all the maturity learned in previous lessons. They work to help others, ideally in a way that can affect the lives of many. Gifted in creative arts and music, they may use that to affect others' lives. 99s intuitively understand how the world works and are at home in any situation. Literally, they can do anything. They may be involved with holistic healing or teach others a more spiritual approach to life. For them, it's time to contemplate what has been learned and prepare for the next step in their evolution. Mentoring is a great tool to confirm what they know.

The Challenge

Confusion	Intolerant	Immoral
Imbalanced	Insensitive	Accusatory
Unreliable	Depressed	Self-centered
Anxiety	Lost	Egotistic
Immaturity	Put upon	Unethical
Helpless	Dependent	Unbalanced
Stingy	Unprepared	Angry
Impulsive	Blaming	Resentful

Self-centered 99s may feel at odds with life. Having seen all aspects of life before, they might rebel at the need to deal with it again. They could get confused by all the possible ways to handle a situation and issues might seem much bigger than they actually are. 99s can become self-centered and ignore people in their lives. Extreme cases can become angry and not accept responsibility for their own failings. They need balance on all levels. It helps to work with others and help them sort out their own issues.

The farmer knows all about farming. He appreciates what he's learned. Now his greatest reward is to help others. He thinks about how to apply his knowledge and experience beyond farming.

TRIPLE Numbers – Important Messages

000 ——————————— Infinite Potential

Zeros added to a number give infinite potential. Without the number, you have nothing.

The Message
You are on the highest path. Everything is in perfect balance. You are doing exactly what is right. The situation you're in has gone full circle and a divine connection is open to you.

The Opportunity
Things are ready to be given form. All things are possible within your highest purpose. Like a guitar amplifier, nothing happens until someone plays the instrument. Then the amplifier makes music based on the musician's intent. Your inner connection is strong. All you need to do is take the right action.

The Challenge
000 can be a reminder. It might be wise to re-establish your inner connection or change direction. Potential can be wasted or misused. Be sure your intent is clear and appropriate.

111

————————————————— **New Opportunity**

Opportunity knocks and what comes next may be very different than before.

The Message
You are entering a new phase or cycle in your life. The change is for your greatest good. Continue along current lines of thought and action.

The Opportunity
Manifestation is a constant process. A door of opportunity has opened and your thoughts can turn into reality very quickly. Monitor them carefully. Shed old habits and patterns that don't serve you. Think about what you want, not what you don't. Energy has accumulated in relation to your thoughts and desires. It will become reality when the time is right.

The Challenge
You may attract things you don't want. Fears or dislikes can become reality. If you aren't pleased with what is on your mind, change it. Thoughts are choices. Choose wisely.

222 —————————————Continue Forward

You are on the right track and will see things start to happen for you soon.

The Message
You are going in the right direction. Things are moving forward and will turn into an actuality. Soon there will be visible results in your life. Trust the process even if you don't have visual confirmation yet. Keep going but stay open to other options.

The Opportunity
Your efforts will bring what you have worked for. A current situation will soon be resolved and work out well for all concerned. Everything you focus on is visualization so stay optimistic and confident. Patience will bring the outcome you want to see.

The Challenge
Fear, lack of faith. Everything you have worked for can disappear before you see it unless you keep your attention on the result you want. Your fears can turn into reality. Stay positive and confident.

333 —————Divine Assistance

Make the right choice and it will help you on your journey.

The Message
The universe and those who guide you support what you're doing. Your choices are good. There may be a decision you have yet to make. Call on assistance for direction.

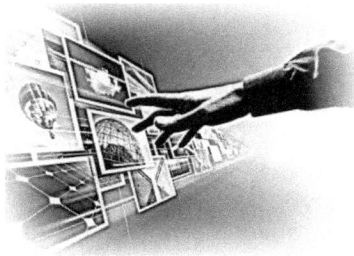

The Opportunity
In some ways this is completion and balance, possibly on many levels. Assistance is available to you when you ask for it. You may have a decision to make and your guides can help you with it. The direction you choose will take you into the future.

The Challenge
A decision may be difficult or have serious consequences. It's important to choose wisely. If you don't listen to your inner guidance, the choice may not be the best one.

444 ———————— Higher Protection

There are forces at work behind the scenes and the situation will get resolved without any effort on your part.

The Message
Higher powers have things under control. Circumstances and events will work out for the greatest good. You are protected. Have confidence as you surrender to what will come.

The Opportunity
Spiritual growth is easy if you stay balanced. Events may be beyond your control but that means that the universe has the reins. Your conscious involvement isn't necessary at this time. Allow the divine in you to take care of the situation. Your move forward will be effortless.

The Challenge
If you mess with what's going on, you will get frustrated and possibly make the situation worse. When fears direct your thoughts, what should be an easy transition may be difficult and unnerving. Let things take their course.

555 ———————————————**Turning Point**

It helps to be ready for change as events and circumstances take a new and exciting direction.

The Message
A time of change is upon you. Life has transformed into a different expression. You need to adjust your thoughts and actions accordingly. Exciting opportunities will emerge.

The Opportunity
Old habits and behavior patterns get replaced by new ones. Now your life will move forward in a new and more suitable manner. Times of change are exciting and provide you with a fresh approach. If you have been planning a move, this can be the time.

The Challenge
Resistance to a major shift creates stress and frustration. Sticking to old behaviors and lines of thinking will cause difficulty for you. Be adaptable or you will be unhappy and disappointed. Life changes and you need to change with it.

666
Material Disharmony

When the situation around you seems like it just can't work, look within for the solution.

The Message
There's a conflict between you and the material world. It could be on a spiritual, mental or emotional level. Change your focus from external things to your inner needs. The physical world will be more supportive if you put less attention on it.

The Opportunity
You've put too much attention on the material world. It is time to get your thoughts back in balance. Your inner needs have been ignored and it's time to change priorities. Listen to that inner voice that keeps you in the perfect balance between material and spiritual worlds. You may be called upon to help another.

The Challenge
Stability may get shoved aside. If you make money and possessions too important, you'll get out of balance. The longer you wait to correct this, the harder it is. The universe will win in the end so you may as well change your approach now while it's easier.

777

—————————————— **Lesson Progressing**

Luck may seem to be with you when you apply what you know.

The Message
You are currently going through an important life lesson. A significant part of the wisdom you incarnated to learn is yours but you must apply it. A period of your life is close to completion. You may find luck is on your side.

The Opportunity
Opportunities can open for you. All you have to do is recognize and pursue them. Miracles are possible at this time. With new wisdom, you can move toward the next lesson in life. You may have to use what you've learned in the near future.

The Challenge
Life will be different for you. If you look into the past for answers, your path forward could be difficult. It may be necessary for you to use newly gained knowledge. Old habits may not serve you as they did before. You will need to change with life as you move into the future.

888 ———————— Impending Change

When a cycle approaches its end, change is on the horizon.

The Message
You've learned something and there's change ahead. Enjoy what you've gained and reflect on what you've been through. It's almost time to move on to the next lesson. Before long, life will be different in some way.

The Opportunity
Life will be different in some way. You have been preparing for something and now you are ready. It's possible that you've changed a long-standing pattern of behavior and will be free of the situations that trigger it. Something may finally seem vividly clear to you. Regardless of the reason, when the adjustment time is past you can enjoy the benefits of what has happened.

The Challenge
There is something you need to learn to move forward. Things could get uncomfortable if you hang on to old patterns or beliefs. Stepping into new thought patterns isn't easy and may require you to re-assess your core beliefs. To feel the flow of abundance, you need to get out of your own way.

999 ———————— Chapter Complete

As you reflect on what you've been through, you see what it means and how to use it in the future.

The Message
You have completed an important phase of your life. It's time to move on. Take the next step in your growth.

The Opportunity
When you successfully complete a phase of life, you can go to the next one. A new chapter opens and all you have learned in the past is available to you. A new direction can be based on what you have gained already or it can be completely different. Either way, you have the benefit of what you have been through to ease the path ahead.

The Challenge
You have reached the end of a phase of your life but there may be something to do before you move on. You may have to prove something through experience. If you failed to learn something from the past, you will have to go through it again before the next cycle of life can open to you. A situation can be harder if you have to repeat it.

PART THREE

Your Potential

Your DESTINY Number – WHAT you were born to do
The total of your birth date

At one time or another, everyone wonders, "Why am I here?"
This question is seldom asked with any hope of an answer,
though. Through the ages people have looked to religion or
seers to help with this. Years of study often provided what they
sought or at least some direction. There is a simple way to look
into this seeming mystery. That way is numerology.

Your destiny number is the date you were born reduced to a
single digit. It shows the life-long mission you are to fulfill and
the kind of lessons you will experience. It affects you from the
day you're born until the day you die. It's the stage on which you
experience life and the strongest single influence.

There are also master numbers to consider. If there is a master
destiny number, you have a higher purpose to fulfill. The master
influence may not be felt at all times but it's always there.

To have more definition for the destiny number, there is also the
driving force behind the reduced number. That is the number
total before it's reduced to the single digit. For example,
December 9, 1975 is 12+9+1975=1996=25=7. The driving force
for the 7 is 1996. June 25, 2006 is 6+25+2006=2037=12=3. For
that date, the driving force is 2037. The driving force is the
unreduced numeric total.

There are several ways to find a destiny number. Higher master
numbers take special calculations so it's important to do all of
them. If there is a master number in any of the calculations it
must be taken into consideration. The more ways you find a
master number, the stronger its influence is.

For our purposes, the month is written as a number so
December 7, 1950 is 12/7/1950. In numerology, the month is
always put first and the year last.

Most people choose one or another way to calculate the destiny number because they feel it's the "correct" way to do it. There is a flaw in this way of thinking, though. It doesn't allow for variations in individuals and what the numbers mean for them. You need to take into account all the types of calculations. Otherwise, everyone with any one of nine destiny numbers is exactly the same.

To show how it can be done, we'll look at a birth date and build on that. Let's use Thomas Edison for the example. His birthday was February 11, 1847. First write the date.

> *2/11/1847*

Below that, write it as a calculation.

> *2/11/1847*
> 2+11+1847=1860=15=6

Below that reduce the month, day and year and add them. If any of them add to master numbers, don't reduce them at this time.

> *2/11/1847*
> 2+11+1847=1860=15=6
> 2+11+ 2 =15=6

Now reduce any master numbers and make another line below that.

> *2/11/1847*
> 2+11+1847=1860=15=6
> 2+11+ 2 =15=6
> 2+ 2 + 2 =6

Finally below that write the individual digits in the birth date as a calculation.

> *2/11/1847*
> 2+11+1847=1860=15=6
> 2+11+ 2 =15=6
> 2+ 2 + 2 =6
> 2+1+1+1+8+4+7=24=6

These calculations only find 11, 22 or 33 as a master destiny number. In Edison's case, there aren't any. The next step is to add some special calculations that can reveal higher master numbers. Separate the year into the century and the year within that century. 1847 becomes 18+47. Add another line above the date to include the month, day, century and year.

> 2+11+18+47=78=15=6
> *2/11/1847*
> 2+11+1847=1860=15=6
> 2+11+ 2 =15=6
> 2+ 2 + 2 =6
> 2+1+1+1+8+4+7=24=6

For the line above that, reduce the month, day, century and year. Remember not to reduce master numbers. If there are no master numbers, you would skip this line and go on to the next line above that. As it is, there is the day (11) and year (11).

> 2+11+ 9 +11=**33/6**
> 2+11+18+47=78=15=6
> *2/11/1847*
> 2+11+1847=1860=15=6
> 2+11+ 2 =15=6
> 2+ 2 + 2 =6
> 2+1+1+1+8+4+7=24=6

There is now a master number as the total. Add one last line at the top with the month, day, century and year fully reduced.

> 2+ 2 + 9 + 2=15=6
> 2+11+ 9 +11=33/6
> 2+11+18+47=78=15=6
> *2/11/1847*
> 2+11+1847=1860=15=6
> 2+11+ 2 =15=6
> 2+ 2 + 2 =6
> 2+1+1+1+8+4+7=24=6

Now the lines can be numbered in the order they affect the person. Line 1 is the strongest influence and line 7 is felt the least. Line 2 is as important as line 1 especially when there's a master number for a total. In many cases, there are both primary and secondary driving forces in each. Consider both these lines for a clear picture of your destiny number. Lines 1 and 3 are the only ones that can show higher master numbers in addition to 11, 22 or 33.

Line 5   2+ 2 + 9 + 2=15=6
Line 3   2+11+ 9 +11=**33/6**
Line 1   2+11+18+47=**78**=15=**6**
         2/11/1847
Line 2   2+11+1847=1860=15=6
Line 4   2+11+ 2 =15=6
Line 6   2+ 2 + 2 =6
Line 7   2+1+1+1+8+4+7=24=6

Thomas Edison's destiny number is 6 with a main driving force of 78. A master number found in any of the less effective lines means it is felt but not quite as much as in the strongest lines. For Edison, 33/6 is a moderate influence. The 33 shows service to mankind. His 6 destiny number meant he could make life better for all. One aspect of the 78 driving force is successful research. Reduced to 15 it means progress and innovation. He was a pioneer of change. Edison developed an electric power generation and distribution system. It supplied power to homes and factories. He was a prolific inventor with 1093 patents in the US and many more in other countries. Some of his inventions that made our lives better are the phonograph, the motion picture camera and the electric light bulb. He introduced large-scale teamwork to make his ideas a reality. In business, he used mass production methods to get things on the market. He even started the first industrial research laboratory. In a sense, he was the pioneer of today's think tanks. Few people can claim to have changed the lives of so many to such a degree.

Until now, higher master destiny numbers were never found. As time passes, there are more people born with a higher purpose in life. These are often shown by higher master numbers. For them, it's a disservice to ignore this.

Gandhi was a fascinating person. He was born on Oct 2, 1869. Notice that his lines 3 and 4 have nothing in them. That's because there were no master numbers for the individual month, day, century and year when they were reduced.

```
Line 5   1 + 2 + 9 + 6=18=9
Line 3   ---
Line 1   10+2+18+69=99/9
         10/2/1869
Line 2   10+2+1869=1881=18=9
Line 4   ---
Line 6   1 + 2 +  6  =9
Line 7   1+0+2+1+8+6+9=18=9
```

Gandhi's life purpose was one of great potential. The 99/9 means divine wholeness, enlightenment and ultimate completion. 9 is honest, ethical leadership. Line 2 has 1881 for a secondary driving force. He was a leader in his endeavors and a successful pioneer. 1881 reduces to 18 to lend even more strength to the 1 and 8 influences. This bears out what he did in life. Gandhi helped India gain independence and led movements for non-violence, civil rights and freedom. You can't find his 99 with just conventional calculations. Without the 99, numerology would not fully show the great man he was. In the section on signature names, there will be more about him.

For another example, take a look at Albert Einstein. His birthday was March 14, 1879.

```
Line 5   3+ 5 + 9 + 7  =24=6
Line 3   ---
Line 1   3+14+18+79 =114=6
         3/14/1879
Line 2   3+14+1879 =1896=24=6
Line 4   ---
Line 6   3+ 5 +  7   =15=6
Line 7   3+1+4+1+8+7+9=33/6
```

Line 7 shows that Einstein's destiny number has 33/6 as a minor influence. The master number isn't as strong as if it was found in any other line. Still, he felt and took advantage of its influence. For him it meant enlightenment and wisdom. His destiny number is 6 for support and selflessness. 114 is the driving force for him. That is practicality (4) and a pioneering leader (1 and 1) so he had the ability to make new or innovative ideas work. Since 114 reduces directly to 6, there is no secondary driving force. There is the secondary driving force of 1896 from line 2 for more insight. This means he was supportive and balanced in business and new ideas. He was against war but worked with the US Government to develop the atomic bomb because he believed that Hitler was going to develop one and use it. 1896 reduces to 24 for a little more information. The 4 and 2 mean practical relationships. He was concerned with the good of the country and saw the people in it almost like a family. He's considered the most influential physicist of the 20th century and is often called the father of modern physics. Einstein used both intuition and logic. He was a man of amazing vision and saw what others did not.

Michael Jackson is another person who was considered a genius by many people. He was born Aug 29, 1958.

```
Line 5   8+2+1+4=15=6
Line 3   8+11+ 1 + 4 =24=6
Line 1   8+29+19+58=114=6
         8/29/1958
Line 2   8+29+1958=1995=24=6
Line 4   8+11+  5  =24=6
Line 6   8+ 2 +  5  =15=6
Line 7   8+2+9+1+9+5+8=42=6
```

As with Einstein, Jackson had 114 for the driving force to make innovative ideas work. He became a dominant figure in pop music. The videos for his songs contributed to the breakdown of racial barriers. With his influence, music videos became an art form and promotional tool. He was a skilled businessman as well as a gifted performer. The Guinness Book of World Records lists him as the most successful musician of all time. In line 2, Jackson had a different secondary driving force than Einstein. His was 1995. That indicated both excitement and balance as a leader and innovator. It reduces to 24 as did 1896 for Einstein and both men had much the same broad view of people. Michael saw his fans as his family. He built good public and professional relationships. He was one of the world's most prominent humanitarians and donated more than $300 million to charity.

There's room for a couple more examples. For these, let's look at the birth dates of Sergey Brin and Larry Page, the founders of Google.com. The factors to consider are in bold print.

Sergey Brin
Line 5   8+3+1+1=13=4
Line 3   ---
Line 1   8+21+19+73=**121**=**4**
         8/21/1973
Line 2   8+21+1973=**2002**=4
Line 4   ---
Line 6   8+3+2=13=4
Line 7   8+2+1+1+9+7+3=31=4

Larry Page
Line 5   3+8+1+1=13=4
Line 3   ---
Line 1   3+26+19+73=**121**=**4**
         3/26/1973
Line 2   3+26+1973=**2002**=4
Line 4   ---
Line 6   3+8+2=13=4
Line 7   3+2+6+1+9+7+3=31=4

As you compare them, notice that the corresponding totals on every line are exactly the same for both men. They were born to fulfill the same life mission. It's no coincidence that they were drawn together. The destiny number is 4. That's practicality, organization and the ability to see how to realize their ideas. They were both good with details and complex plans. The main driving force is 121. That shows pioneering leadership with a partner. The secondary driving force for them is 2002. That would indicate very high potential to work in partnership. Their names reveal even more but here's a quick rundown. Brin is a pioneer in business ideas. Page is creative in practical business deals. For partners in a whole new type of business, it doesn't get much better than this.

The destiny number shows a person's potential, the best case scenario. Famous people have generally lived up to that. It doesn't mean everyone will, though. The thumbnail explanations given here are just to show what the numbers mean and how they work together. You could write a whole book on any one of them but that's not the main purpose of this book. Use your head and intuition together. Read the full definitions and see how they work with other influences. It helps to look at people close to you to see how they apply. There are other factors that add to the overall picture of the person, too. There will be more about that in the section on names.

Lines 1 and 2 are almost equal in how they define one's life. In many cases, there are both primary and secondary driving forces in each. Consider both these lines for a clear picture of your destiny number.

What Your Destiny Number Means

1 is your DESTINY number
The strongest life path is a 1 destiny. It's about independence and to make your own way. You stand on your own and have faith in yourself, your ideas and your potential. You are to learn about self-reliance, leadership, originality, courage and confidence. This is the destiny of the pioneer and like a pioneer, you are self-sufficient and self-motivated. You venture forth in a totally new direction and lay the groundwork for others to carry on. Unlike other paths, this one is free of the restrictions that limit so many. At times, you may have to exert yourself to accomplish goals. You can then draw on your considerable inner strength and determination. Stay balanced, though. Be cordial and develop a genuine interest in the needs of others.

2 is your DESTINY number
Your main focus is to develop relationships. This path is how to get along with others. That means partnerships, marriages, friendships and alliances of all kinds. It's also the relationship you have with your surroundings or even yourself. There will be lots of close associations in your life. That can be with a spouse, partners, employers, employees, co-workers, work groups or professional contacts. You're patient, charming and tactful. Subtlety gets what you want. It's easy for you to bring balance

between opposing forces or conditions. You make the perfect diplomat or peacemaker. You work well as part of a team where cooperation and finesse are needed. Strong-willed people provide direction for your abilities. The best role for you is to be the quiet force behind greatness.

3 is your DESTINY number

Creativity and imagination is the base of this destiny. It's to develop self-expression in all its forms. You're at home in any activity that needs new ideas and innovation. With a good command of language, you have highly tuned social skills and like to interact with people. Any creative outlet is good for you. You can be a good artist, writer or entertainer. It's easy for you to communicate ideas on any level from vocal to visual. People like you and find you both entertaining and inspiring. You can add new life to any conversation. Because you are so versatile, it may be hard to stay focused on a single idea until it's matured. Pace yourself and channel your energy. When you carry a project through to completion, your success is assured.

4 is your DESTINY number

You're responsible and hard-working. With this life path, you have a knack for details and order. This destiny is about how to apply yourself and complete projects. You're logical, not ruled by emotion. It's your opinion that things worth having require good, honest work. This is a strength because it helps you to get a job done when others may feel overwhelmed. In addition, you enjoy a challenge. You are dependable, practical and ready to serve in any capacity that helps get a project done. Be careful because not everyone has your abilities. Others may wear out before things are finished if pushed too hard. Temper your enthusiasm with patience. You lead by example so be sure to set a reasonable pace. With your nose to the grindstone, you can do well at anything you take on.

5 is your DESTINY number

Life is interesting, exciting and full of variety. Situations fade away or turn into something new. Your life is full of freedom and change. You may travel or work in a travel-oriented profession. When events take a surprising turn, you adapt quickly. What seems like a disaster to some could be an opportunity for you.

Try to not get too tied down or you may feel stifled and ineffective. You excel at communication and sales. Others find you entertaining and full of ideas. You can put in a full day and be ready for an evening out. Don't expect others to keep up your pace because they probably can't. See projects through to completion. That will bring great successes to you. Keep your bags packed and be ready for whatever comes your way.

6 is your DESTINY number
The compassionate provider. A 6 destiny is about home and family. This path represents the love among family members, especially between parent and child. You want this in your own family and at work. In business you feel it with your employer or employee. It could also be the relationship between you and a client or customer. You're fair and trustworthy. Those who can use your help are attracted to you. At times you'll have to put the needs of another ahead of your own. Common sense and communication skills can put you in the position of an advisor whether for a family member or a head of state. Give guidance where you can, but don't try to live for another. Sometimes a person needs to go through their own learning experience. Be as fair as possible and you will always do right by others.

7 is your DESTINY number
Mental and spiritual activities power a 7 destiny. You like to think and work things out on your own. You are more suited to quiet research than group efforts. Social events and family affairs may feel like a burden at times. You're quite interested in the meaning of life. Science and philosophy offer a chance for you to explore that. Gifted with inner peace and confidence, solitude gives you a chance to look inward for answers. Where others seek approval, you have confidence in your own abilities. Knowledgeable in your area of interest, you usually get the last word in. You don't need to aggressively attack life because opportunities will always be there if you're open to them. Others need to express their opinions and can be a good resource for you. Listen to them. You can benefit from their insights and knowledge.

8 is your DESTINY number
An 8 destiny is about success and prosperity. Business will bring success if you're willing to put out the effort. The financial world is good for you and you feel an affinity with it. Vision and determination combine to give you good judgment. You're polite and can make powerful allies in key positions. If you stay ethical, honest and trustworthy, you'll get a reputation for good business sense. Find opportunities to help those around you. When you're tolerant and fair with others, they will give the results you want. This path is about much more than just money and business. Prosperity pertains to any part of life that provides a feeling of success. You can have a wealth of friends who make your life richer. Family can be a source of great accomplishment. You may simply enjoy reaching a goal. Stay focused on the desired result. Success can be yours in any way you want. You just need to put in the effort and build something.

9 is your DESTINY number
This is the end of a master cycle of nine incarnations. Opportunities come from what you've learned in the previous eight life lessons. It's a good time to complete unfinished business from previous lives. Your broad philosophical outlook, high ideals, optimism, honesty and compassion make you a good humanitarian or leader. You could even be a world leader if you put your mind to it. You're creative and can communicate with anyone. You understand people and what motivates them. In the capacity of a judge, you're capable of great understanding and fairness. You can now improve on some part of what you already know. Consider people who are brought into your life. You may be able to take care of karma with them. Take the time to appreciate all you are and what you've learned. In this, you prepare for the next master cycle. Get ready for the next phase of growth and where those paths will take you.

11/2 is your DESTINY number
An 11 destiny is enlightened leadership and selfless service. This could mean life as a spiritual leader or a diplomat. Your accomplishments may put you in the public eye. There are times when you display an impressive depth of vision. You are easy to get along with and enjoy time with others. You're welcome at gatherings and can keep people entertained for

hours. Highly creative, you enjoy art, music and beauty in all forms. People are attracted to you for guidance and will follow when you set an example. You could be a very good inspirational teacher. You see the spiritual qualities in everything. You may even work as an intuitive. As such, you would help people realize their higher purpose. Intuition and insight carry you through situations that would incapacitate others. You're a dreamer but one who sees the overall scope of a situation. You can come up with good plans and ideas but others may need to carry them to completion.

The full potential of the 11 includes the energy of the 2. That represents relationships of all kinds. You may feel drawn to the arts and music but the greatest potential is found with the 11. When you understand the value of 2, it can power the higher purpose of genuine leadership. Be sure to read the definition of the 2 destiny.

22/4 is your DESTINY number
A 22 is both practical and idealistic. You can turn any idea into a reality. This destiny has great power and influence. You see the full scope of a project in detail and can carry out large-scale plans from start to finish. You get great results when your skills are used to help others. This path has lots of potential but it needs to be channeled constructively. This isn't a problem, though. You can organize just about anything. You bring spirituality into practical activities or carry practical ideas to a spiritual height. As well, you can make a spiritual concept into a practical plan so many can benefit from it. On this level, you can make a major difference in the world. For you, patterns show where others see only chaos. You're a superb diplomat that can negotiate with anyone. Life is most rewarding when you work for the benefit of large numbers of people.

There's a very practical side of this destiny in the reduced value of the 4. Self-discipline and application gets results for you. The 4 gives you a solid foundation to pursue the higher aspects of this life path. Read the definition of the 4 destiny. It's the driving force behind the 22.

33/6 is your DESTINY number

The 33 destiny is to work on both spiritual and worldly levels. At times, you may have to put the needs of others above your own. You could be a spiritual leader, master teacher or community figure. You can unify groups and help them get greater results than otherwise might be the case. This could be a lifetime of sacrifice but that doesn't mean to do without. It just means that you'll help others on their paths. If this is done out of compassion, it will be a rewarding life. If your energies are wasted on hopeless causes, you'll be nothing more than a martyr. You can heal others and give them new life. Just the same, you can do that with an organization that is devoted to the benefit of many. You may be drawn into health care, especially when it's associated with natural cures and herbalism. You know there's no difference between spiritual and worldly pursuits. Awakened to your own divine light, you can help others in any capacity you choose.

The influence of 33 must be balanced. 6 provides that in the way of family or work groups. Your path is to provide service and the real reward is to help others on their worldly journeys. Read the definition of the 6 destiny. It will help you carry out your higher purpose.

44/8 is your DESTINY number

Life is the physical expression of one's inner being. The Universe provides for all on the material plane. You like to do this in practical ways. Through business and service, you help those who have less than enough. Vision and spirituality are the tools you have to do that. You apply spiritual values and practices to accomplish your goals. With your help, others can appreciate the vast bounty of the Earth. Instead of just necessities, you can give the needy a way to be self-sufficient. You may teach farming or other necessary skills that elevate people out of dependence. Your work could make you a hero to many. You like to show that the application of spiritual values offers higher living standards. It can provide much more than just necessities like clothes, food and shelter. Because of your efforts, others may take their place in society and stand proud in their own right. You do this because it's the right thing to do.

The influence of the 8 provides the skills of power and prosperity. The 44 puts those to practical use through hard work and focus to a specific end. The 8 gives you the skills necessary to carry out your plans. It provides a good foundation for higher achievements. See the definition of the 8 destiny as well.

55/1 is your DESTINY number

This is the way of an inspired leader or master guide who helps large numbers of people. The 55 destiny is to share and work with others for the greater benefit. You may be drawn to an occupation that needs high energy and considerable knowledge. If travel is required, that's all the better for you. Freedom in all forms is close to your heart and you may work to provide that for others in some way. With groups of any size, you alter what is there or find a whole new direction for them. This can be in exciting new ventures that haven't been tried or even thought of before. The size of the group or corporation doesn't make any difference. You may teach others how to make a difference in the world. You can communicate with people on whatever level is needed so they can get your message. Public attention and fame may come your way as a result of your efforts. That's not too important to you, though. What you care about is the result.

When the pace of the 55 gets too intense, the reduced value of 1 can provide a temporary refuge. That, however, is high energy as well. 1 is the pioneer influence and that gives you a way to explore and find solutions. Then you can go back into the high-stakes activity of the 55 again to put them to use. Be sure to familiarize yourself with the 1 destiny.

66/3 is your DESTINY number

Universal love is the real strength of this destiny. You have a spiritual approach to life and want the best for everyone. People's true nature is expressed in their earthly lives. A change in worldly behavior makes a change in one's spiritual being. Likewise, a change on a spiritual level brings change in a person's life. You're fully aware of your connection to the infinite. You are responsible and trustworthy. With your approach, you would be well placed as a spiritual leader. You'd be concerned for the well-being of all, your followers or not. The role of parent or guardian has a different meaning for you. Family perception is strong and drives your successes. You're right at home as a family member or a world-class peacemaker. Insight and intuition helps you make high ideals a reality. As a politician, you could make the world a better place for all. As long as you focus on the benefit of all concerned, this path should be highly rewarding.

The 3 can help you with the higher meaning of 66. If you develop good social graces and communication skills, you can be more effective. You can get creative with solutions and put your own mark on anything you do. Read the definition of the 3 destiny to know more about how that applies to you.

77/5 is your DESTINY number

A shaman uses higher energies and his intent to make changes in the world. Your purpose is much like that shaman or applied spiritualist. You can bring new things into being from universal sources. This ability is a tool you can use to help other people. You do it easily and may forget that not everyone can. You understand people and can identify their strengths and issues better than others. It's not your way to interfere or give strong advice. You prefer to guide people by example unless they ask for assistance. Then you open up and give them all they can handle. You have access to so much that many people are not ready to hear or see. For those who are ready, it's your purpose to help them reach their full potential. For those who aren't, you will gladly help them prepare for what's to come. Be careful to use your talents and powers for the benefit of others.

You can also enjoy all the travel, change, freedom and excitement the 5 affords. It's a good foundation and offers much to help with your higher purpose. Don't get caught up in it completely, though, or you will miss your true calling. Read about the 5 Destiny and see how it can bring exciting opportunities for you.

88/7 is your DESTINY number

There is a common belief that spirituality and worldly success can't co-exist. This is inaccurate. Everything is spiritual and business is no exception. Your destiny is to show that. Others might choose a life of business over one of spirituality. You like to show that spiritual ideals are part of all activities. True spirituality is unselfish and helps all. It's not self-oriented, but it doesn't mean one should deny worldly desires. As an advisor, you can guide business development or help people work through issues. You know wealth is just a tool, not an end in itself. You're capable of great growth and understanding. As with all master numbers, you may be in a position to help people. You could be able to support them in pursuit of their goals. That would promote success for you, as well. There's no better reward than to help people and achieve greatness doing it. The key is to use spiritual methods for the benefit of all.

Underlying 88 is 7. It's introspective and self-confident. With this influence, you can use your own resources. It can help you relax and regenerate for the next step. Meditation and intuition help you access the knowledge within you. That way, you can manifest things into the physical world. Read the definition of the 7 destiny to see what support it offers.

99/9 is your DESTINY number

A 99 destiny is the proving ground for physical life. It is the culmination all previous life lessons. Everything you've learned may be used now. This path is to prove what you know through experience. It's also time to provide opportunities for others. Use all the spiritual tools at your disposal. You can help and inspire through art or musical expression. You may choose a life of humanitarianism or be in a position of power. You can choose any level of being to accomplish your mission. This path can take almost any direction, as long as it's done with concern for others. It also is time to experience optional lessons not possible before. You've been through it all and have genuine compassion for others in their lives and lessons. Take what the universe offers and express it in your life. Then you complete the journey and prepare for the next step in your evolution.

99 reduced is 9. This is the only master number that is made of two expressions of the reduced number. It provides a foundation of honesty, integrity and trustworthiness not found in other numbers. This is the final cleanup prior to the next level of growth. Read the 9 destiny as it is very applicable for you.

PART FOUR

The Tools You Have

Your FULL NAME – The Three Main Influences

Names and words mean something to your subconscious long before you consciously interpret them. It happens in an instant. Even after your conscious interprets what was said or read, your subconscious still controls what it means in your life. When you hear a word or name, your subconscious reacts to it and that affects how you act. It in turn affects how others respond to you. It's a two way exchange that for the most part goes completely unnoticed.

The name your parents gave you can't be changed. It's on your birth certificate and that's that. Your subconscious uses it to direct a lot of your actions. You can legally change your name or add one but your birth name is always the same. It's the strongest influence. Even with a legal change of name, it still has a very pronounced effect on you. Other names just add to that influence and create a shift in your life.

Your destiny number tells what you are to accomplish. The elements in your name show how you go about it. The three main influences in your name are, 1) the way you work, 2) how you perceive yourself and 3) what others see in you.

To work with a name or word, you have to convert everything to numeric values. Refer to the following the chart for the values.

1	2	3	4	5	6	7	8	9
A	B	C	D	E	F	G	H	I
J	K	L	M	N	O	P	Q	R
S	T	U	V	W	X	Y	Z	

The numbers in 'Jennifer' are J=1, E=5, N=5, I=9, F=6 and R=9. The values of the vowels go above the letter and consonants below.

```
5     9 5
J E N N I F E R
1   5 5 6   9
```

Next, put the total of the vowels above that and the total of the consonants below. Also put the total of all the letters off to the right of the name.

```
            19
      5     9 5
    J E N N I F E R =45
    1  5 5 6   9
            26
```

Reduce the vowels to their lowest value. Then do the same for the consonants.

```
      1               Total vowels reduced
     19               Total vowels
  5     9 5
J E N N I F E R =45=9  Total all letters - (45 reduced to 9)
1  5 5 6   9
      26              Total consonants
      8               Total consonants reduced to a single digit
```

All the letters in "Jennifer" reduces to 9. The total of the vowels reduces to 1 and the total of the consonants reduces to 8.

In the name "Luther" it would look like this. L=3, U=3, T=2, H=8, E=5, and R=9. The totals are as shown.

```
     8               Total vowels - single digit, nothing to reduce
   3     5
L U T H E R  =30=3   Total all letters written as a master number
3  2 8   9
     22              Total consonants - (master number)
     4               Total consonants reduced to a single digit
```

The letters in "Luther" total to 30 which reduces to 3. The vowel total is 8. The consonants total to the master number 22. Add another line with it reduced to the single digit, 4.

Hyphenated names are treated as one and the punctuation gets no value at all. The name, "Marie-Louise" is done this way.

2	Total vowels reduced to a single digit
11	Total vowels reduced to a master number
38	Total vowels
1 95 639 5	
M A R I E - L O U I S E = 55/1	Total all letters written as a master number
4 9 3 1	
17	Total consonants
8	Total consonants reduced to a single digit

"Marie-Louise" has two master numbers. The total letters is 55 and the total vowels is 38 which reduces to 11.

For a full name, Bob Dylan is a good example. He was born Robert Allen Zimmerman. The most important influence is his birth name so that's what we use. His stage name is an additional influence but the one he was born with still has the greatest effect in his life. There will be more on additional names later in the book.

Each individual name has the totals in parentheses. How the total for the full name is done can also be put in parentheses.

```
 6  5          1  5        9   5   1
R O B E R T (=33/6)  A L L E N (=17=8)  Z I M M E R M A N (=49=4)  = (33+17+49) 99/9
 9  2  92        33  5      8  4 4   9 4  5
```

Above the full name total, put the reduced value of each name and the totals. Use a "/" in place of an equal sign so it doesn't look like a total of the vowels.

```
 6  5          1  5        9   5   1      /(6+8+4) 18 = 9
R O B E R T (=33/6)  A L L E N (=17=8)  Z I M M E R M A N (=49=4)  = (33+17+49) 99/9
 9  2  92        33  5      8  4 4 9 4  5
```

Below, put the reduced total of each name with any master numbers not reduced. Precede it with a "\" instead of an equal sign.

```
  6  5            1  5          9   5   1        /(6+8+4) 18 = 9
R O B E R T (=33/6)  A L L E N (=17=8)  Z I M M E R M A N (=49=4)  = (33+17+49) 99/9
9  2 92           3 3  5        8  4 4  9 4  5    \(33+8+4) 45 = 9
```

Now total the vowels above each name. Total the consonants below.

```
   11                6                15
  6  5            1  5          9   5   1        /(6+8+4) 18 = 9
R O B E R T (=33/6)  A L L E N (=17=8)  Z I M M E R M A N (=49=4)  = (33+17+49) 99/9
9  2 92           3 3  5        8  4 4  9 4  5    \(33+8+4) 45 = 9
   22                11               34
```

Reduce each total, vowels above and consonants below. Make two lines, one with any master numbers not reduced and one with them reduced.

```
   2                 6                6
   11                6                6
   11                6                15
  6  5            1  5          9   5   1        /(6+8+4) 18 = 9
R O B E R T (=33/6)  A L L E N (=17=8)  Z I M M E R M A N (=49=4)  = (33+17+49) 99/9
9  2 92           3 3  5        8  4 4  9 4  5    \(33+8+4) 45 = 9
   22                11               34
   22                11               7
   4                 2                7
```

Now total the vowels and consonants across to the right. Reduce them to single digits or master numbers.

```
   2                 6                6            = 14 = 5
   11                6                6            = 23 = 5
   11                6                15           = 32 = 5
  6  5            1  5          9   5   1        /(6+8+4) 18 = 9
R O B E R T (=33/6)  A L L E N (=17=8)  Z I M M E R M A N (=49=4)  = (33+17+49) 99/9
9  2 92           3 3  5        8  4 4 9 4  5    \(33+8+4) 45 = 9
   22                11               34           = 67 = 13 = 4
   22                11               7            = 40 = 4
   4                 2                7            = 13 = 4
```

There are three totals for vowels, three for consonants and three for the total name. It's good to do all of them to find any master numbers. If master numbers didn't matter, you could get by with just one calculation for each.

Here's what it all means. The vowels tell the ambition number, the consonants show the impression number and the total of all letters is the expression number. There will be more on these in the sections that follow.

```
6                6              = 14 = 5    ┐
6                6              = 23 = 5       Ambition
6                15             = 32 = 5    ┘
 5         9     5    1          /(6+8+4) 18 = 9  ┐
_E N (=17=8)  Z I M M E R M A N (=49=4)  = (33+17+49) 99/9  Expression
3  5          8  4 4  9 4    5          \(33+8+4) 45 = 9  ┘
 I1              34             = 67 = 13 = 4 ┐
 I1              7              = 40 = 4       Impression
 2               7              = 13 = 4    ┘
```

The strongest lines to contain a master numbers are the ones that aren't reduced. The driving force is the unreduced total of the strongest lines.

```
6                6              = 14 = 5    3rd
6                6              = 23 = 5    2nd
6                15             = 32 = 5    1st (Strongest)
 5         9     5    1          /(6+8+4) 18 = 9  2nd
L E N (=17=8)  Z I M M E R M A N (=49=4)  = (33+17+49) 99/9  1st (Strongest)
3  5          8  4 4  9 4    5          \(33+8+4) 45 = 9  3rd
11               34             = 67 = 13 = 4 1st (Strongest)
11               7              = 40 = 4    2nd
2                7              = 13 = 4    3rd
```

In Bob Dylan's birth name, the strongest line for expression number totals to 99. Since it's a master number, it is typically written 99/9. The secondary driving force is 18 (99=18=9). The master number has the greatest effect since it's in the strongest line position. His ambition number is 5 with 32 as the driving force. 4 is his impression number and the driving force is 67 with a secondary one of 13.

Here's a quick look at what the influences can mean. Properly done, these should be much more in-depth. 99/9 as an expression number shows the use of higher values in life. In the

1960s Dylan was considered an informal leader of social change. He was involved in US civil rights and anti-war movements. His songs were full of political, social and philosophical meaning. He was influential in American culture. There are recognizable similarities to the 99 in Gandhi's destiny number. With Gandhi, it showed what he was born to do. With Dylan, the 99 guided how he went about his life. His stage name, "Bob Dylan," is 30=3. That means creativity to a very high degree. It gives direction to the way he uses the 99 influence. It shows he could be an outstanding singer and song writer. He has received numerous awards and been inducted into the Rock and Roll Hall of fame, the Nashville Songwriters Hall of Fame and the Songwriters Hall of Fame.

Two or more middle names are counted as one. Prefixes, suffixes and titles like "Dr.", "Esq.", "Jr.", "II", or "2nd" are not counted unless written on the birth certificate as part of the name. Numbers in a name are added to the total but not included as either a vowel or consonant. The same rules apply to words when used in a business name, slogan, ad campaign or similar use.

There are times when a consonant is considered a vowel. Perhaps the most common is "Y". The name, Bryan is this way. It's pronounced the same as Brian. There are times when other letters are used as a vowel, too. "W" and "J" are sometimes counted as vowels and there may be more. Silent letters are given the value they would normally have. The "K" in know is just one example.

The three main influences are covered in this book. They are the total of the vowels, the total of the consonants and the total of the whole name. As with the destiny number, if there's a master number in one of the other lines, it is taken into consideration as a lesser influence. In those cases, some people will feel its effect and others won't. Often you can notice the influence once you know it's there.

Your EXPRESSION Number – HOW You Work
The total of all the letters in your name

Every mechanic has a toolbox. The tools in it determine how he gets a job done. Your name is like that toolbox and the *expression number* shows how you approach life. To calculate it, total all the letters in your full name as it is on your birth certificate. Reduce that number and you have it.

The expression number shows your abilities and career potential. It tells how you interact with the outside world. It's how you solve problems, react in situations and deal with others to get what you want.

If there's a master number in your expression, you have an additional, higher way you can function in life. Found in the strongest position shows that it will most likely affect the course of your life. In the weakest position, you may never feel it. The potential is still there if you choose to take advantage of it, though.

George Washington and Thomas Jefferson both had master numbers in their names. They both lived up to the fullest potential of this.

```
  5 6   5         1   9    6        /(3+4) 7
G E O R G E [=39=3]  W A S H I N G T O N [=49=4]  = (39+49) 88/7 EXP
7   9 7           5  18  5 7 2  5
```

88 gave Washington the ability to master what came to him in life. He knew self-control and how to overcome temptation. This helped him in the battles for US independence. He was responsible and used higher values to motivate and command his men who thought him to be divinely guided. Washington was known to pray for guidance before each battle. His men were devoted and wanted him to be the king of America. He didn't

give in to the temptation for personal power, though. Instead, he worked to make the United States the best possible place for future generations. When he became president, he did all he could to help the country grow. He strongly believed in the principles that the United States was founded on.

```
   6   1              5   5   6      / (4+8) 12 = 3
T H O M A S [=22/4]  J E F F E R S O N [=44/8]  = (22+44) 66/3 EXP
 2 8   4   1          1 6 6  9 1   5      \ (22+44) 66/3
```

66 is universal love and family values. To Jefferson, the country was his extended family. Although he was a wealthy land owner, he saw the dangers in a system of government run by the wealthy. He wrote the Declaration of Independence almost by himself. That and the US Constitution were designed to protect the people of the country and insure that all people got the same chance in life. An interesting fact is that his destiny number is the same as his expression number. He was perfectly suited to fulfill his life mission. He was devoted to the country. Jefferson is often thought to be one of the greatest U.S. presidents.

A number that ends with a zero (30, 40, 50, etc.) shows that the influence can be stronger than otherwise. As an expression number, it shows the ability to get great results. A good example of this is John Lennon.

```
 6          9    6          5    6      /(2+6+11/2) 19/10/1
J O H N [=20=2]  W I N S T O N [=33/6]  L E N N O N [=29=11/2]  = (20+33+29) 82 = 10/1 EXP
 1   8 5    5   5 1 2   5    3   5 5   5      \(2+33+2) 37 = 10/1
```

Lennon was another popular figure who made a great success of life. The 10/1 shows that the potential of 1 was increased and could easily take a strong direction. 1 is leadership and innovation. The driving force is 82 for alliances or partnerships in business. Lennon started a band called the Quarry Men which evolved into The Beatles. The group was his idea and he certainly was the leader. John was a pioneer and his music was

94

often as unique as he was. His rebellious nature showed in his music and manner. A peace advocate, he was active in the anti-war movement. Some of his songs were even adopted by the movement as anthems. The Nixon administration even tried to get him deported for his views. Many considered him a musical genius. There are some similarities to Albert Einstein and Michael Jackson in his birth date. Rolling Stone magazine dubbed him as the 5th greatest singer of all time. After his death, he was inducted into the Songwriters Hall of Fame and the Rock and Roll Hall of Fame.

What Your Expression Number Means

1 is your EXPRESSION number
A pioneer at heart, you'll step into the unknown, see what's there and forge something new. With complete confidence in yourself, you branch out from normal lines of thought. Often your solutions are very different than what others come up with. You can design a new device or implement fresh ideas. Like a good scientist or researcher, you're independent of the self-imposed limitations most people feel. This gives you total freedom of thought and action. Your ambition helps you carry out ideas. With superior leadership ability, you can lead others in the pursuit of dreams. Be sure to finish existing projects before you start new ones. In your pursuit of life, remember to develop a genuine concern for the needs and interests of others. When you show people the way to success, you gain insights that propel you forward, as well. Although it isn't the only way, you can be a mentor and simply offer direction. That could provide the balance you need to be successful. Be that pioneer. Blaze a path for others to follow. It doesn't mean you assume the responsibility for anyone. You just provide the direction for them.

2 is your EXPRESSION number
Relationships provide you the greatest comfort. You make the perfect parent or spouse. People mean a lot to you and you love to work with them in any capacity. Although able to strike out on your own, you prefer to share experiences and interests. You like strong-willed people because they can provide direction. Rather than be the center of attention, you would rather quietly

make things work out. Subtlety really works for you because you have the patience to apply it with charm and tact. You can sense the feelings of others and easily mediate disputes. It suits you to be the force behind the throne, consoling or encouraging as needed. Your subtle ways help you achieve your personal goals as well as propel others to success. Look after your own interests so you don't get shorted. Fears can disrupt your sense of balance and symmetry. Keep your dignity and self-esteem high. Harmony is important to you. Turn a little of the love you have for others inward. This will help you to maintain a positive attitude. Channel your energies for the benefit of all, yourself included.

3 is your EXPRESSION number

Creativity in any form moves you to the very core. You are inventive and full of new ideas. You tap into the universal storehouse for ideas and give them form in the physical world. All that ability carries over into your whole life. Originality shows in your work and projects. You're versatile and can turn anything into a thing of beauty. All of life is your canvas. You approach it with a positive, artistic flair. There are always new ideas to act on. Stay focused on existing projects so they get done. You are entertaining and enjoy social interaction. Creative ideas often do more than just provide the immediate satisfaction of self-expression. They can offer avenues to success as well. Look for ways to use your talent that have a practical use. When you start to feel negative, perform a few charitable acts. That will help shift your attention back where it belongs. You have an infinite source to draw from. Honor the abilities of others and pass on some of your ideas for their benefit. Learn to be humble and others will truly value your input.

4 is your EXPRESSION number

Good, honest work is your way to fulfillment. You love practical solutions. If there's an orderly way to approach a problem, you'll find it. You are efficient, results oriented and capable with a good eye for detail. Hard-working and patient, you're content to do whatever gets results. People can depend on you to carry a project to completion. You're right at home in situations that require concentration and diligence. Emotions don't get in your way. You're good with your hands and can do just about anything you set your mind to. Loyal and responsible, you can be trusted to get things done when you say. Be aware that you may outwork others without realizing it. Few can keep up with you so be patient with those who don't have your tenacity. You tend to be conservative in appearance and manner. There is a good chance that you drive a brown or gold car and like vehicles that have a useful purpose. You may get a little too focused on the worldly aspects of life. It's good to meditate or simply take time to relax and think. A walking meditation may be what you need to stay balanced.

5 is your EXPRESSION number
Change, transformation and variety make your life an exciting one. You easily adapt to new conditions. Travel feeds your need for adventure. When a project takes an unexpected turn of events, you make the best of it. Your mind is quick and sharp. You can assess complex situations fast and come up with solutions almost immediately. An occupation with a fast pace or one that requires you to make snap decisions may be perfect for you. You're a good-natured optimist with a quick wit. You like to interact with people. As a good judge of human nature, you can fit in anywhere with any type of people. You're strong and courageous in unknown situations. As often as not, your adaptability pulls you through. Few people throw themselves at life the way you do, though. Let them act as they see fit. It's easy to be critical of people when they show more caution than you. To them, you may seem egotistical or judgmental. Step out of the spotlight now and then. Be sure to cultivate a little humility. Encourage others and be supportive. Don't always expect them to follow your lead. In your pursuit of excitement, you may get a little reckless. Exercise some caution, especially where others are involved.

6 is your EXPRESSION number
Gifted with natural protective instincts, you're sensitive to people's needs and situations. You're very understanding and sympathetic. Comfortable in any relationship, you know how to deal with other people's problems. You're knowledgeable and can easily communicate ideas to almost anyone. You can be a

great advisor or mediator. This could be in the home or in an official capacity. Gifted with an acute sense of right and wrong, you want to see others treated fairly. People feel your concern and open up to you. They also see you as knowledgeable and feel you can keep their secrets. You would do well in a service-oriented profession. You have a great capacity for love. Don't hold back while you wait for someone special to enter your life. At times you may seem a bit superficial but when you show an honest interest in others, they soon see that you are genuine. At times, it may seem to you that others take credit for your work but that's more a perception than reality. People often need to find their own way. Know when to let them do that or you may seem meddling. Let your sense of harmony be the guide and success will follow.

7 is your EXPRESSION number

You're a perfectionist at heart. Where others just want to get a job done, you like to be thorough. You study and gather information to fully understand a situation. Analytical fields like psychology and science are a good fit. Your desire for the best solution can help you as a researcher or investigator. You're not one to join organizations or teams. Instead, you like to meditate and look inward for answers. This could lead you into the occult. As likely, you could be attracted to astrology or numerology. Your natural dignity could make you seem like a loner but that doesn't bother you. One of your strengths is to be happy with your results. Only after you have solved a problem will you share it with the world. It's beneficial to be generous to the very people you feel don't measure up to your own strict standards. You can understand them more and get a better perspective on humanity. If you seem odd or neurotic to people, it's just because they don't understand you. Cultivate more open relationships with people around you and you will be more centered in your own strengths. Put aside a little time to develop a genuine concern for the needs of others.

8 is your EXPRESSION number

The business world is your playground. You're right at home with business plans, accounting systems, financial plans and production schedules. Any position where you can work toward a tangible goal is good for you. You understand people and what motivates them. This makes you a good manager. You're efficient and self-motivated. There is great potential for you in any executive position. You're a natural diplomat and can make powerful friends and allies in strategic positions. You like to have lots of contacts and know how to get the most out of networking. Don't get too concerned about what others may say or do. With faith in yourself, you can excel at anything. It is good for you to donate to charities. That shows your subconscious that there is plenty available for you and opens the way for even more success. Besides just income, you'll find that the operations side of business can be rewarding in itself. Don't get greedy about what you have. Watch how you treat subordinates and don't be domineering or self-centered. Pay attention to how your actions affect others. If you're aware of their needs you'll reach your goals the fastest.

9 is your EXPRESSION number

With strong drive and energy, you can do anything. The 9 expression has a balance of influences. As the completion of a cycle, it includes a little of all the numbers. With so much ability, you're most comfortable when in charge. Like any good leader, you consider the needs of those under you. You're a true humanitarian with high ideals and do well in positions that can benefit all of humanity. You could be successful in public service, possibly as a judge or politician. Somewhat of a romantic, you tend to be a little emotional at times. You also have a strongly artistic side. If you aren't an artist, you appreciate those who are and may collect art or donate to museums. There may be times when you feel that others aren't listening to you. You have good information and insights but can't be too forceful with your message. That can turn people away from your cause. Get detached from your emotions and be practical. The universe is a loving place and supports the pursuit of your goals. Let ethics guide you and life can be most fulfilling.

11/2 is your EXPRESSION number

Intuition and vision help carry out your life purpose. You're a gifted leader. This could put you in the role of an inspirational teacher, an intuitive or a spiritualist. People sense that you have a high level of being and are attracted to you. When in charge, you display higher values, love and diplomacy. Natural insight helps you along in life. You can get your point across to most people. You're a creative person and often show pure genius in your chosen field. At some time, you may be publicly recognized for your work. You like to help large numbers of people and can forget to take care of yourself. Be sure to set aside time to see to your own needs and desires. Intuition guides you when logic fails. You may seem a little eccentric to others but that's just because you are unconventional. Visualization comes easy for you so concentrate on the results you want. Finish existing projects before you start more. It helps to have practical people around to help see that projects get completed.

When the power of the 11 gets too intense, you can fall back on the 2 to relax and recuperate. This is more about partnerships and relationships. It's easy for you to maintain meaningful relationships in your work and daily life. You're a good mediator and love to bring harmony and balance to discordant situations. This provides a level of balance for you. You still need to develop discipline to reach your goals in a timely manner, though. Keep your focus on the end result at all times. Also read the definition of the 2 expression.

22/4 is your EXPRESSION number
You're a master organizer and grasp the whole scope of a project. You see patterns where others only see disorder. The first thing you do is identify key concepts or functions. Then you organize it in detail. When you begin work, you stay with it from start to finish. You have a fresh approach with totally new solutions to problems. Immensely capable with your hands, you can take on any job. All you need is a little time to pick out the essential aspects and organize them in your mind. Then you do it as well as anyone and in many cases, better. You're confident and know your own abilities. You bring spirituality into the practical world or take practical ideas to a spiritual height. As a leader, you like to work alongside those under you. You're generous and considerate. In the role of a mentor you can give

others direction in their work or life. You quickly manifest things into reality so choose your thoughts carefully. Focus on what's positive and you'll bring more of the same. It's important to get direction from your destiny number. Success could be yours on a wide, even international, level.

At times the 22 expression is too much high energy. You then need a change of pace with the 4 vibration. In this, you become more detail-oriented. You find practical solutions to complex problems. The 4 helps you be less emotional about your work and wait until the right time to implement your plans and ideas. You are loyal, responsible and dependable. Your conservative nature allows you to blend in with your surroundings. Watch that you don't get too focused on material things. To stay balanced, meditate or walk and allow your inner thoughts to surface. Don't be too cautious or you'll miss the incredible opportunities of the 22.

33/6 is your EXPRESSION number

Firmly anchored in the power and harmony of the universe, you can help people fulfill their higher purpose. Your gift is to give support on higher levels. It's obvious to you that there's no difference between spiritual and Earthly pursuits. You are ready to help on whatever level people are ready. Wise and patient, you do this at their most comfortable pace. Life as a health intuitive or spiritual leader could be for you. You're concerned for the welfare of the world as well as individuals. There is real potential for you as a master teacher who helps others to grow and better themselves. The more levels you work on, the better you like it. You may help animals and those who have them in their lives. This could be as an animal communicator or healer. You are at home in the health care field. In that, you're most interested in herbalism or alternate cures. You're kind, generous and compassionate. You often work on a worldly level because "purely spiritual" work doesn't really exist. When you guide people in daily life it also helps them spiritually. To switch between the two, you simply change your focus. The result is the same.

When you need a break from the strenuous pace of the 33, there is the reduced vibration of 6. It lets you work on more worldly issues. That lays the groundwork for spiritual growth. With a good sense of right and wrong, you can steer others along their paths. People open up to you readily, eager to hear what you have to say. There's no need to get immersed in their drama, though. Offer solutions but don't take their problems personally. Help them work out their own answers and you will work at the most fulfilling level. Freely give the great love you have to others. This opens you to accept help, as well. You have to know how to receive in order to give.

44/8 is your EXPRESSION number

There is a point where spiritual and material planes come together. This is true of all occupations and activities. You can merge these on a wide scale. You have a direct link to higher guidance and see the divine in everything. You make that an integral part of all you do. Others learn from the example you set. Able to focus vast resources, you can get spectacular results. You work best on a large scale and for the benefit of many. You know that the natural world is not only necessary for our growth but our continued existence. You'd like to see it kept clean and nurtured for future generations. You see the spirituality in business and really prefer to use it to provide plenty in the physical world. A path you may take is to insure that mankind has its material needs taken care of. You're particularly suited to help people provide for themselves. In your eyes, the world is the physical expression of our inner selves. You see the spiritual nature of material projects and want to show that to others so they may grow and prosper.

The intensity of the 44 is too much, the 8 puts your focus on business and finances. This is very helpful when you work on a world-wide endeavor. It allows time to make the practical aspects of a project flow smoothly. You can draw on your business sense and use it for the greater good. Your communication skills are acute. You fit well in almost any situation and can mediate or negotiate as needed. Keep your attention on higher goals and use the 8 to get meaningful results. You may choose to work in the business world and build your wealth. With material success, you can then focus on the greater needs of the planet.

55/1 is your EXPRESSION number

With your determination and intuition, you make a natural leader. You can forge ahead to success when you have a group or team to work with. Able to remember things in detail, you can recall them when needed. You are able to think on multiple levels and find a strength or weakness. As a military commander, you can organize men and resources to gain the best advantage. Others follow you, confident that you know what you're doing. You eagerly look for new avenues, places or ways of thinking. You function well in unknown situations where you must adapt to the unexpected. Borders are not obstacles to you. Instead, you think in terms of area advantages and limitations. You can make inroads where others would feel overwhelmed. Travel is fine with you. A move in the pursuit of a project can be a pleasant addition to the whole experience. Where leadership would burden many, it allows you total freedom. You are wise enough to utilize the assets provided by the individuals on your team. Consider their well-being in your plans and you are unstoppable.

It is beneficial to fall back on the 1 influence to renew before you head out again. At those times, you work fine by yourself. Your personal strength and confidence rejuvenates you like nothing else. You are independent and determined. Often your solutions to problems are totally new and original. The 1 brings out your self-sufficiency. New projects are easy to start and you enjoy the challenges that come with them. As with the 55, include others in your pursuits. Take a genuine interest in their needs and concerns. If you mentor someone as a way to pass on your knowledge and experience, you would pick up a different perspective. That in itself could provide insights into the course for your own life.

66/3 is your EXPRESSION number

The Universe is your home and you answer to the highest power in it. You are a provider with an affinity for family. That can mean your spouse or it can be all of mankind. Regardless of the scope, you want the best for everyone. You are loyal, stable and responsible. Able to get along with anyone, you're quite popular. Work associates, subordinates, customers or suppliers all feel they get special treatment from you. Your spiritual approach to life makes you a good spiritual leader or counselor. You like activities where you can make the home, homeland or home world a better place. Whether you approach it as a profession or not, you are a natural teacher. You present an idea so anyone can understand it. As a peacemaker, you're second to none. You can negotiate a peace treaty or settle a dispute between children. Outgoing and expressive, you may be drawn to a life of service in diplomatic circles. You could also work for a large corporation that benefits the whole planet. Don't get involved in something that helps just a select group. With a focus on the greater good of all, your life is most fulfilling.

The reduced vibration of 3 can be relief from the pace of your higher purpose. Your creative side is necessary to reach the goals you've set as a 66. It helps you relax and charge your batteries for the next big step in your plans. Use your imagination to come up with new ways to get things done. When life seems a bit tense or out of balance, doing a few charitable acts will help you regain your proper footing. Your creativity is inexhaustible. Pass a few ideas on to others for their benefit. Be humble and let others share the credit with you.

77/5 is your EXPRESSION number

This is the most intelligent and inventive of all the expressions. You are gifted with a pure mind and could be a prophet, sage or spiritualist. Like a shaman, you apply mystic powers to real life situations for positive change. With your ability to manipulate the physical world, you could work as a remote healer. You realize and appreciate your connection to the infinite. New concepts can come through you from universal sources. World events don't interest you unless they pertain to spirituality or growth. The world around you gets attention when you're affected but that's not where your heart is. Instead, you prefer to go inward and enjoy the riches there. Then you apply them in the physical world. Your ability to grow spiritually is beyond the comprehension of most people. You really understand people and their needs. Where possible, you like to share your vast understanding so others may grow. You know when to step aside and let them learn on their own. You offer guidance only when needed. You're friendly and polite. This helps you be a good leader and teacher. When in the public eye, your charisma is a great asset. You can do well in entertainment, motion pictures or other creative fields.

When a change of pace is in order, you can enjoy the change and variety of the 5. Travel may be part of your life. The travel, however, could be astral journeys. They can take you places within that few ever suspect exist. You adapt quickly to new ideas and situations. Transformation is almost second nature. Don't get too involved with the pleasures of the world or get hooked on sheer change. Share the spotlight sometimes. Give others a chance to express themselves without judgment or criticism. A little self-assessment now and then will help you stay on track. You can enjoy personal growth while you help many with your insights and counsel.

88/7 is your EXPRESSION number
Your life is a proving ground for the application of spiritual principles. This is true of any activity from corporate work to driving a truck or the family BBQ. For you, it doesn't matter what it is. You are the master disciple. You've been through many, many lessons in past lives. Now you have the opportunity to show what you've learned. It's time to apply spirituality in all things. Your entire life is the stage for this. There will be many opportunities and choices for you. When everything in your life resonates at a spiritual level, you can have great prosperity and success. Both of these are found in all of life, not just your income. Good friends or family are prosperity. When you redecorate your home, that's a success. There are many chances for you to achieve perfect balance between the seemingly opposing forces. You can use intent with responsibility and careful planning. To get the results you want, use power and control with discrimination. You are able to build a self-made fortune and may do so if it suits your needs in this life. You may help others do it. The examples you set are important, too. Set some to be proud of.

7, the reduced vibration of 88, is good for a shift of focus. With that, you can research solutions and develop courses of action. You can tap into inner resources and then apply the principles to any activity. Meditation can help you rejuvenate and get ready for what's next. Save time to build relationships. That grounds and centers you. Help those who need to improve their standards. When you help others grow, they help you as well. You gain perspectives you wouldn't get otherwise. This works in business or personal life. If you encounter obstacles, go within. Find the best solution and apply it.

99/9 is your EXPRESSION number

Finish up old issues and prepare for your next step forward. This expression is both completion and preparation. It's time to prove all you've learned and fine-tune anything that's less than perfect. There may be challenges from past lives to deal with now. Life could bring others who have their own unfinished business with you. This is a good time to set things right. You can be gracious and answer the needs of another just to help. You may be drawn to holistic healing. You see the human body as the temple for the spirit that should be cared for with love and compassion. This applies to your own health as well as that of others. You're creative and can be quite artistic. This may be how you choose to connect with people. You can create beauty that touches others on levels they're totally unaware of. You are honest and ethical. Others feel this in you and trust your judgment. Although you may sometimes feel a little out of place in the physical world, you are very much a part of it. Your insight and level of spiritual growth carries you through times when logic isn't enough.

99 is two nines that work together. The single 9 is a more worldly side of the same energy. Your leadership and organizational skills are suited to everyday activities. At times, it may seem that others don't listen to you. You have good information and insights but your forceful nature can turn people away from your cause. Be less insistent with your message. You can choose which level of existence to experience in this life. The greatest fulfillment is with the higher path. Without it, life

may seem less complete. If you ignore the worldly path, life could be too intense. Immerse yourself equally in both and you'll find the best balance. Either way, life can be rewarding and enjoyable.

Your AMBITION Number – How You SEE Yourself
The total of the vowels in your name

What do you want? That may sound like a simple question but to properly answer it, there are some false 'desires' to eliminate first. Discount things you need like a job, a home, food, clothes, education, etc. Then toss out what you've been taught you should want by your parents, church, society, government, television, friends and associates. Lastly discard everything you have interpreted from life experiences. Now consider what remains. Those things are what motivate you on a very basic level. A few may be like some you dumped but that's OK. They are the true desires you were born with.

Sounds like a daunting task, doesn't it? There's an easier way. The *ambition number* reveals how you would like to see yourself, not influenced by what you believe is possible. It indicates why you make the choices you do and what the "ideal you" wants and strives for. It's also what you would like to project to others, although not necessarily what you *do* project.

The ambition number comes from the vowels in your full birth name. Add them and reduce the total. If there is a master number it will steer you toward a higher purpose in life.

The ambition is what you came into the world with. It shows what really motivates you. That may get buried by artificial desires but it's what really matters to you. The ambition gets tempered by the other numbers in your birthday and name.

We saw what Michael Jackson was born to do. Here's how he saw his role in life.

```
   6              2              7          = 15 = 6
   6             11              7          = 24 = 6
  15             11              7          = 33/6 AMB
 9   1 5       6   5          1    6
MICHAEL[=33/6]  JOSEPH[=28=1]  JACKSON[=20=2]
 4  3 8   3    1  1  7 8      1  3 3 1  5
```

The strongest line has 33/6 as the ambition number. For him, the effect would be strong. 33 shows his dream was to bring advancement and awareness to those in need. The 6 means he would be compassionate for others and want the best for them. He would use higher values in his efforts to help. As a humanitarian, he donated millions to combat drug & alcohol abuse and help disadvantaged children. He donated proceeds from several of his songs and one musical tour. He supported 39 charities and established his Heal the World Foundation. In all, he gave hundreds of millions of dollars to help those in need.

The ambition number can offer insights into why someone feels and acts the way he or she does. See how yours holds true for you.

What Your Ambition Number Means

1 is your AMBITION number
With your strong will, you really want to be the leader. You want to come out ahead in all situations and are most comfortable in the lead. Ambition and confidence motivates you to do your best. You prefer to deal with people who like to follow an established lead. Like-minded people want to run the show, too, and conflicts can arise. Also as the leader, you have a chance to express your originality. The pioneer in you can find a solution when situations seem hopeless. You often have new ideas faster than you can process the old ones. For that reason, you may get impatient with the speed at which things get done. Make allowances for those who help you. They always function

at their most efficient level and you can slow down easier than they can speed up. The unknown doesn't bother you at all. You like a good challenge, especially when it's something no one has done before. You get courage from the determination to get a job done. Although it isn't in your basic nature, you can be an excellent support individual. With that perspective, your leadership is greatly enhanced and you are even more effective.

2 is your AMBITION number

All relationships have the potential for harmony and you want to see that realized in them. You like cooperation and partnerships of all kinds. Any good relationship pleases you. You see the great potential in pooled ideas and efforts. You're a great mediator and when people disagree, you want to help them find the perfect solution to their situation. You're capable of great love and you understand people. In turn, you also need to feel the same from them. To share and cooperate with others gives you the most comfort. You feel people are more important than worldly things. At work, your salary is just a side benefit of your occupation. You prefer to focus on the relationship aspects of it. With your love of people, you'd rather help someone realize his or her goals than just go after your own. In fact, your real goal is to help others. You measure success by how well you get along with people. You have a genuine love of home life. You are attracted to occupations that let you be useful in those areas. When you know the end benefit of a project, you can choose the best way to use your talents.

3 is your AMBITION number

The creative process, in all its aspects, is your forte. You love all things of beauty and all forms of communication. Your fertile mind comes up with fresh ideas all the time. For you, self-expression is paramount to any other consideration. You have the ability to choose any means to express your vast imagination and creativity. One way to do it is with words. Equally, you may use art as a way to convey ideas. You can do anything with your hands. Sometimes it helps to have new things to focus your attention on. You listen to others' ideas for inspiration. Any good idea stirs your imagination. Often a good one will bring even more of them. Nothing is less appealing to you than mundane repetition of anything. In your pursuit of artistic expression, you may get bored with existing projects. Unless you stay with them until they are done, you could get frustrated or confused. You like to be the center of attention. People appreciate your wit and the way you tell a story. An audience helps you to relive what you're talking about. Your enjoyment is then multiplied many times over.

4 is your AMBITION number

Most important to you is an organized life with firmly set rules. You pay attention to details and work out solutions based on solid facts and order. You're thorough and a logical thinker. If something has a practical use, you value it. Otherwise, you just aren't interested. You get a great deal of satisfaction from hard work and results. You like to see a definite plan with a defined payoff. All aspects of a project need to be agreed upon before any work starts, though. Honesty and ethics are very important to you. You have no patience with deviousness or deception. You're dependable and always meet deadlines. People can count on you to be on time and get a job done well. In return, you want the same from others. Your home and job mean a lot to you and you take pride in both. When you commit, you are loyal and devoted. A patriotic individual, you'll dedicate your time to a good cause. Although you are patient, you tend to discount ideas that aren't practical. There aren't many details that escape you. You may take a little longer at the start while you formulate a good plan. In the end, the time proves well spent.

5 is your AMBITION number

Freedom is as necessary for you as food or shelter is for others. You need to be able to travel and experience different things. Borders or restrictions don't stop you. You love change and are the first to welcome new situations or ideas. Mundane or repetitious situations bore you. You may change careers now and then to just experience something new or different. As adaptable as you are, you can learn a new job in a matter of weeks. In a couple of months you can work right alongside those who have spent their whole lives at it. You take unfamiliar situations in stride. Travel fits your sense of adventure and need for variety. You take life on its own terms and enjoy it. It really satisfies you to master a new challenge. Social activities for you are another way to experience different situations. Good physical stamina lets you live at a breakneck pace. That's fine since you love every minute of it. You have a superb memory and can recall anything when you need it. Physical sensations give you relief from your ever-active mind. As long as you don't overindulge in sex, food, drugs or alcohol, you can easily do anything you choose.

6 is your AMBITION number

It's your nature to seek harmony and balance in all situations. You feel that home and family should be nurturing and supportive. If they're not, you'll do all you can to make them so. You're committed to a perfect relationship with your spouse, children or siblings. You are friendly and easy to get along with. A sense of responsibility and love moves you to give guidance where you can. You're a good listener and can see all sides of any issue clearly. People trust you with their inner secrets. They count on you to help settle disputes and know you will find the best solution for everyone concerned. Family for you is much more than just relatives. It's anyone you're closely involved with. It could be people at work or the community where you live. When someone is in need, you are there to help. Motivated by high principles and idealism, you do the best you can in any situation. You want everyone to be happy and like to be a matchmaker. You're confident in your ability to deal with others and can talk to anyone about anything. As an arbitrator, you find good solutions between individuals, businesses or governments. You are most effective when you're not involved with their situations.

7 is your AMBITION number

One of your greatest resources is the wisdom and spirituality within your own being. You're much more confident in your ability to work alone than with others. People's failings don't bother you. You just go about business without their involvement. Facts and thorough research mean more to you than hunches and theories. You're self-sufficient and work best at your own pace. You like to gather as much information as possible before you start anything. Then you want plenty of time to meditate and mull things over. It takes time to analyze information so you can extract useful bits of data. For this you need privacy. You are intelligent but the intrusiveness of the world can upset your train of thought. Your surroundings need to be peaceful and comfortable. When you're satisfied with the result, you'll share it with others but not before. You tend to be a perfectionist and appreciate quality in all things. It doesn't work for you to actively seek out opportunities. The best approach, which is your preference anyway, is to let them come to you. Relationships aren't needed for your well-being. You feel complete on your own. You will take heed of others' ideas, though, and can improve your own effectiveness by integrating them with yours.

8 is your AMBITION number

Everything you undertake is well thought out with a definite goal in mind. When you put out an effort, you want it rewarded. You like to stay busy and have a clear goal. On any project, you constantly re-assess what results you'll get. With an aptitude for management, you always seem to end up in the lead. People recognize your business sense and follow you without question. You know all about running a business. Any company or organization operates efficiently and smoothly with you in charge. You take pride in being punctual and always meet deadlines. You intuitively know what people want. Because you address their needs, you usually get your way. The task at hand is always most important to you. It's essential to you to finish a project before you start a new one. You know there are always more opportunities. If you pass on one, another will take its place. You like to be in control. When you react emotionally, it really bothers you. You have great physical and mental stamina. It satisfies you to work as well as, or better than, those around you. You tend to not be power-hungry or materialistic. It's your basic nature to stay balanced and keep on track.

9 is your AMBITION number

As a humanitarian, you would like to see quality of life improved for all. You are strong with drive and like to be in charge. As a leader, you're very effective. Ideally, you would be the head of a service-oriented occupation or activity. Honesty and idealism are important to you. Guided by high ethics, you do the best possible for all concerned. You are trustworthy, creative and independent. People feel this and trust you to do the right thing for them. In business, you like straightforward dealings. There's no place for deceit or hidden agendas where you're concerned. You're fair and understanding. This makes you good as a judge or political leader. Many of your decisions are made intuitively and they're usually right. You tend to be somewhat of a perfectionist but when that's tempered, it just makes you more effective. You're orderly and clean up as you go. You like to see current projects completed before you move on to the next one. You know what you want and like to set goals. A romantic by nature, you may react emotionally to what life brings your way. When you keep your emotional reactions in check, there's balance in your life. You'd like to see everyone have that balance.

11/2 is your AMBITION number
Rather than deal with the practical aspects of everyday life, you would prefer to make a difference in the world. You really want to help people. You strive for the ideal expression of everything you do. In your occupation, you seek a higher form of achievement. The more you can work for the ultimate benefit of others, the better you like it. Products or services need to improve life for others or help to clean up the environment. If you amass a fortune, you will most likely use it to finance projects that benefit many. You want to find the ultimate partner, one that understands you and is down-to-earth. Ideally, such a partner would deal with mundane tasks and basic necessities for you. Your ideal spouse would be one who shares the same goals and will work alongside you to accomplish them. Leisure activities are best when shared with others. You also like to be in the public eye. What puts you there doesn't matter that much. More important, you like recognition for your accomplishments.

2 is the underlying strength of 11. It's the framework that supports the higher influence. Capable of great love for others, you need to feel loved and understood by them. You want to see harmony in all relationships and partnerships. To be part of

a successful team or work group really satisfies you. You could
easily end up as the driving force within it. You are comfortable
under another's direction, whether at work or in the home.
Either is fine with you as long as it works. You like to cooperate
with others and share in their pursuits. For you, material needs
are secondary to how people get along. You have a genuine
love of home and home life. You may be attracted to
occupations that let you be useful in those areas.

22/4 is your AMBITION number
Fully aware of your own potential, you want to use it on as large
a scale as possible. You would like to devise a practical way to
make the world a better place. A noble cause appeals to you
and you'd love to be the one to organize it. You can carry out
large-scale plans from concept to fruition. Gifted with vision, you
can see a project in detail before you start work. Then you will
work up a detailed plan and see it through, one step at a time,
until completed. All obstacles have a solution and you take care
of them as they appear. With your attitude, you can accomplish
just about anything. You want to have the power, people and
resources at your command to achieve far-reaching results.
Your capacity to apply what you know is, at times, almost
inconceivable to others. When you need an expert but one isn't
available, you can become that expert, at least well enough to
get the job done.

It isn't always possible to work on global issues. The practical
skills of 4 have more every day uses. Most important to you is to
lead an organized life with firmly set rules. You're thorough and
a logical thinker. You appreciate practical solutions based on
solid fact and order. Detailed plans give the results you want to
see. You like to formulate a good plan of operations before you
start a project. Overall, the time is well spent. You're honest and
have no patience with deviousness or deception. Waste goes
against your sense of economy. You believe in hard work with
definite rewards. Once you commit to something, you like to see
it through. Your home and job are very important to you and you
take pride in both.

33/6 is your AMBITION number

Rather than to just provide basic necessities, your dream is to bring advancement and awareness to those in need. You know there is spirituality in all things. This is where you are well-suited to help. Your compassion and understanding go far beyond that of most people. You don't care much about material needs. Instead, you see the higher learning that the world offers. For you, money can be a tool that frees one to concentrate on higher concerns. Life situations offer a way to learn something. You know the body is a visible expression of one's inner self. Most only want to heal the body. You want to help people grow spiritually so they no longer need their physical problems. Natural or herbal cures could give you a way to help others that you would enjoy. Another area that would be rewarding for you is to work as a spiritual counselor. As the latter you could help people work through the underlying cause of physical problems. You willingly sacrifice for others when situations warrant it.

Since you can't always work to fulfill the higher calling, the 6 adds to the power of 33. With a love of balance and harmony, you want to create ideal situations. You love family and home life and will do all you can to make it nurturing and supportive. You're committed to your spouse, children and siblings. Your family may be an extended one with many members. You are friendly and easy to get along with. Guided by high values, you are often called on for guidance. In your desire for supportive interaction, you are a good match-maker. You like to see disputes get settled. Others tend to count on you to be there for them. You like to live up to their expectations.

44/8 is your AMBITION number

There is a divine power in everything. You see it and want to apply its higher principles to improve the lives of all people. You have a spiritual focus that directs your energies. It's obvious to you that spiritual values can make great changes in the world. You like to use them to pursue goals and want to be an example of how this gives the best outcome in life. To provide things such as food, shelter, clothing and medical aid pleases you. More so, you like to help people be self-sufficient. You want to motivate them so they can take care of themselves in the future. You love nature and mankind's place in the scheme of things. You have visions of abundance for all. On a global level, you want to provide a higher standard of living for everyone. Ideally, you would help others see the world for what it is, a physical expression of our inner selves. You know this insight would improve every part of their lives. You are a quantum visionary and given the opportunity will focus vast resources to achieve notable results. You want to insure that the worldly home of mankind is kept clean and nurtured for future generations.

Additional strength comes from the 8. On a practical level you're motivated by prosperity and material rewards. You have a keen aptitude for management. In group situations, you like to be in charge. You want to see a business or organization operate as efficiently as possible. You're punctual and take pride in it. You also like to get your way. Results-oriented, you want to finish a project before you start a new one. It bothers you a lot when you react emotionally. You have great physical and mental stamina. It satisfies you to outwork work anyone else.

55/1 is your AMBITION number
There are people who make new concepts available to everyone. You're one of them. You like social projects that benefit lots of people. An interest in spiritual or metaphysical things gives you direction in how to carry out your dreams. You prefer to take an existing project in a whole new direction. If there isn't a good one available, though, you'll start one. The universe is your home and you understand how it works. You know all belief systems follow the same basic principles. In a very real way, you're at home with any kind of people. You see the true meaning in their customs. This enables you to step in and work alongside them to promote their goals. You're able to present new ideas in a way that doesn't conflict with their beliefs and traditions. You enjoy the infinite variety in life and can turn almost any situation into an opportunity for change and growth. Total freedom comes when you live your ideals. You want your life to be a positive example for all. Public recognition for your efforts is an added boost. Life is exciting and you like to be free from the restrictions, self-made or otherwise.

New situations and infinite variety are normal for you. You want to work for the benefit for others and the underlying influence of 1 helps with this. You're independent and like a challenge but it's important for you to succeed. You are a good leader and prefer to deal with those who like to have a set course. New ideas come to you faster than you can process the old ones. At times you feel impatient with the speed at which things get done. You appreciate what others can do for your projects. When you let them work at a pace that's comfortable, they really can help you get your projects finished.

66/3 is your AMBITION number

Others may be concerned with achievement or personal development. You, however, want to see other people fulfill their life mission. When you help others reach their goals, you reach yours in the process. You want everyone to function at their best. For this, you see the need for a supportive environment. It pleases you to help people have that. You want to see the home, homeland or home world support everyone. You work for the benefit of all, especially with children and family. You like to bring harmony between opposing parties. Where there is disagreement, you want to step in as the peacemaker. Your dream is to see all people, groups and nations get along with each other. Not only do you take a spiritual approach to life, you want it to be a part of everything you do. You want to see mankind live in accordance with higher forces. You feel accountable to the highest spiritual source, however you perceive it, and your loyalties are to that over all other considerations. You like to meditate and experience higher consciousness. You really like to serve others in spiritual matters and may find great satisfaction as a spiritual leader.

3 is the creative influence behind 66. You love the creative process in all its forms and like to share your ideas with others. Friendly and entertaining, you like to have people around you who enjoy your wit. The way you tell a story or relate an experience is always clever. With a fertile mind, you always have fresh ideas. You love all things of beauty and may use art as a way to communicate in addition to the written or spoken

word. For you, self-expression is paramount to any other consideration. You're good with your hands. That gives you the freedom to choose just about any way to express your vast creativity.

77/5 is your AMBITION number
Universal connection is a big part of your life. Things of a spiritual nature help bring harmony for you. You want to find practical uses for the insights you have. It's all the better when you can apply them for a tangible result. You like to think of yourself as one who can access infinite knowledge. From that, you gather useful information to be used by, or for, others. You want to bring into being new concepts that can help people. With the basic inner desire to help, you may work as a shaman or mystic. Shamanic or other inner journeys can be as natural for you as a trip to the store is for most people. Chances are you've gone through considerable growth yourself. You like to be a missionary of transformation. Though you have the ability to change people's lives, you don't interfere or take on anyone's problems. Instead, you make yourself available and will step in when asked. You're not as concerned with worldly issues as you are individual situations. Ideally, you would like to help all of mankind grow as individuals. You are a humble realist and appreciate public attention for the way it can boost your efforts to help others.

The energy of 5 gives the strength of change and adaptability. New experiences are welcome in your life. You like adventure and travel fulfills your need for excitement. You're bored by mundane or repetitious situations and may change jobs now and then just to experience something different. It's easy for you to master new challenges. You take life on its own terms and enjoy it. With any change, you simply adapt and keep going. New people in your life mean more variety, and you like that. Your good physical stamina allows you to live at a breakneck pace and love every minute of it.

88/7 is your AMBITION number
Many think wealth is the greatest goal of business. For you it's a way to prove higher principles. Great results happen when you use these principles for worldly goals. You want to master

abundance. This is done with a good balance of spiritual and worldly means. You enjoy business and all that's associated with it. You are at home on any level from telephone sales to large commercial ventures. You're as honest and ethical as you can be. You know what's needed for success and can achieve just about anything. With the use of pure intent you can bring things into being. You use that ability with responsibility and careful planning. Not just for material rewards but because it is for the benefit of all. In addition to material success, you need higher values to be really fulfilled. A master at self-discipline, you can transmute temptation into something to help reach your goals. Ideally, you want to gather a core of capable people to help you along the way. Everything you do is for the mutual benefit of all concerned.

The secondary force of 88 is 7. This guides your daily activities. You like a private life, separate from business. A quiet and peaceful home atmosphere lets you meditate and get ready for more. Then you can go back to work refreshed and ready to make deals. Your work place also needs some privacy so you can think and mull things over. Confident in your own abilities, you trust your own solutions over those of others. You would rather let opportunities come to you. That's fine since there usually seems to be a plentiful supply of them to choose from. Personal relationships don't work that well for you because they cut into your valuable time.

99/9 is your AMBITION number
99 is the final step to prove all worldly lessons. You're in the unique position to help anyone who needs and wants it. You're wise enough to know this is a great responsibility with no material gain for you. In your opinion, the body is the temple of the Spirit. You have a genuine concern for the well-being of others. You love life and may choose to work in holistic healing or a similar field. In all situations, you like to show a perfect balance between spiritual and worldly qualities. You like all aspects of life and can literally do anything. You may express yourself in music or art. If so, there is often an otherworldly quality to your work. Art for you can be a way to communicate

with others. You can affect them subtly and they won't even know it. Your own potential is so obvious to you that you take it for granted. Fully aware of your higher purpose, you expect to make it a reality. You understand people since you've been through every kind of situation yourself in past lives. You want to see others overcome their obstacles but you also know when to not interfere. You are there for them when they are ready.

The reduced vibration of 9 is very similar. You make a good humanitarian and want to help others improve themselves and enjoy the many wonders life has to offer. Strong with drive, you like to be in charge. You are trustworthy, honest and independent. For this reason, you make a good judge or political leader. Many of your decisions are made intuitively. You like order and are not one to leave a project unfinished. You want to complete things that need to be done. You know what you want and like to pursue goals.

Your IMPRESSION Number – How OTHERS See You
The total of the consonants in your name

A ship has propellers that move it forward on its journey. They're completely out of sight and to a casual observer, the ship would seem to move along without any means of power. Your subconscious is like a propeller. Unseen, it interacts with the world and other people to carry you along your life path. This is shown by your impression number. It's how others perceive you and, to a degree, how they react to you.

The impression number is the total of the consonants in your full name. It is reduced the same way the expression and ambition numbers are.

Name calculations aren't just for people. The name of a business, an item or a location have the same influences. Everything is done the same. For an example of the impression number, here's the USA.

```
   5        3 9 5              1 5         6        1  5 9 1
 T H E(=15=6)  U N I T E D(=28=1)  S T A T E S(=12=3)  O F(=12=3)  A M E R I C A(=32=5)
 2 8         5 2  4           12 2  1       6        4  9 31
 10          11               6            6        16              =49=13=4
 1           11               6            6        7               =31=4
 1           2                6            6        7               =22/4
```

The impression number is 4. There is a driving force of 49 with a lesser influence of 22. People see the USA as a place to have a balanced and orderly life. Those with an eye to move here would expect a fair deal. The 22 shows that anything is possible with a practical plan. A sense of national pride is strong. The expression number is 99/9 for ultimate completion and a gateway to a new life. The influence of adventure and transformation is seen in the birthday. (The real birthday of the country is 4/30/1789, the day Washington was inaugurated as the first president under the constitution.) The driving force for that is 140. That's the high potential of a responsible pioneer. No wonder so many have immigrated over the years.

The following definitions are what the numbers mean from the perspective of an observer.

What Your Impression Number Means

1 is your IMPRESSION number

People see you as a strong leader that gets the job done. Not only do you make great plans but you jump right in and carry them out, too. You tackle jobs that others are reluctant to take on. Seldom do you follow normal guidelines. Instead, you're innovative and set new trends. You always seem to have good ideas. Where others see only one way to do something, you are there with a better way that no one has thought of before. People are often awed by your ability to move forward with any kind of project. You initiate new programs with ease and set a course of action that others can pick up where you leave off. You're confident and self-reliant. Others would describe you as courageous. They trust you to work through any difficulties that crop up. Co-workers and associates see you as a capable self-starter. You get going early and seem to have limitless drive and energy. If you're self-employed, people expect you to be successful. As part of a team, those in charge know they can count on you to get the job done without any input on their part. They expect you to rise to the top before anyone else.

2 is your IMPRESSION number

Tactful and charming, you have the uncanny ability to bring harmony to just about any situation. You do best when you work closely with others. This can be in a work group or any kind of relationship. You can get along with anyone. With tact and understanding, you get the best from people. You pay close attention to plans and agreements. People expect you to get results when others might fail. All your needs seem to be met almost without any effort on your part. The way you bring order and symmetry to life is almost mystifying to many. Where others battle with people and situations, you gently work out agreements. To some, it seems a mystery how you keep your life so well balanced. You can make friends with people who don't seem to fit in with others. You see their potential and know how to work with them. When disputes arise, you're always in the middle with solutions that work for everyone. Employers and workmates all see how well you can get people to focus on a task. With good ability to understand people, you place them in positions where they do best. Patient and empathetic, you always seem to know what people need. When someone lacks direction, you can give appropriate guidance. You can bring stability to almost any situation.

3 is your IMPRESSION number
With seemingly limitless energy and imagination, you always have fresh ideas. Whatever you do and wherever you go, people notice your talent. You always put your own special, even artistic, twist on everything. In your chosen field, you often show creative genius. You seem to radiate creativity and self-expression. Even if your occupation isn't an artistic one, you manage to make it seem like one. You're good with your hands and can turn anything into a work of art. It looks to others that you can do just about anything. You're imaginative and intelligent. You have a sixth sense when it comes to addressing a situation, even if it's not familiar to you. Friendly and outgoing, you're a natural entertainer. People like to have you at parties and other functions. Because of your wit and manner, there's always a circle of people around you smiling and laughing. You're kind and optimistic. The opposite sex is attracted to you. They might even see you as a sex symbol. You're fashionable and attractive. You always know what to wear and how to carry yourself.

4 is your IMPRESSION number
Logical and efficient, you always build a sound foundation for everything you do. You plan a detailed, orderly course of action before you ever start work. Then you tackle each step in the most suitable order. You're down-to-earth and a strong, loyal part of the lives of your family and friends. People know they

can count on your help when it's needed. They see you as a very practical and patient person. You may drive a practical car or wear Earthy colors. Obstacles don't bother you. You just work out a solution and move forward. You don't get emotionally involved in things, either. You surprise people at how clearly you see what is needed to do a job. You enjoy hard work and like to get rewarded for your efforts. People like the fact that you don't complain about what needs to be done. You simply apply yourself and put the task behind you, something many wish they had the ability to do. Although others may have difficulty keeping up with your pace, they're impressed with how much you can accomplish. You are a very welcome addition to any project.

5 is your IMPRESSION number

Everyone sees you ready for adventure and excitement. All of life seems to be your playground and you can tackle it smiling. You never seem to be overwhelmed at what life brings. Always on the move, you have limitless energy and an appetite for the unknown. You adapt to change in an instant. Travel pleases you. The different cultures and situations never seem to faze you. When needed, you can meet any situation with ease. At social gatherings and public functions you're right at home. You can carry on a conversation with a variety of people. You express ideas so anyone can follow what you mean, no matter what their background might be. Complex ideas and concepts are easy for you to understand. You look youthful and attractive. You move quickly and your mind is always active. You lose interest with repetitious tasks. Where others like things that are tried and true, you'd rather do something no one has done before. You can make the best of any situation. You seem to have the ability to turn anything into an opportunity. For leisure you always have something interesting to do and are up for any new adventure. It can easily be something no one has done before. Caution doesn't need to be part of it, either. It just has to be interesting.

6 is your IMPRESSION number

The whole world is your family. Whether on a personal or community level, you treat all people with a friendly and caring manner. This means anyone from close friends and blood relatives to workmates or other groups of which you are a part. You can get along with anyone and certainly do with those around you. Everyone gets the same treatment. Where most have a few significant people in their lives, you seem to have many. People find you easy to be around. They also expect you to keep personal information to yourself. Your home is comfortable and all who enter are welcome. At work, your work space is harmonious and relaxing. In work groups, you always manage to see that all parties get along and work together. You're great with words and people listen to what you have to say. When advice is needed, you always know what will help. If someone has problems in a relationship, you are there to help both sides find a workable solution. You are responsible and dependable. In any situation, you can be counted on to help negotiate or mediate if needed. An idealist, you manage to end up in occupations that work for the greater good of the community.

7 is your IMPRESSION number

Self-confident, you rely on yourself rather than others. People respect your ability to work by yourself. You often come up with new information or answers that others may not find. This is because you don't let preconceived ideas influence the way you think. You're very capable and can be left alone to work out solutions. You explore all possibilities before you draw conclusions. People may see you as detached or aloof. On the surface, it would appear that you have a sage-like detachment from the problems of the world. Those more familiar with you know that you do care. You just don't express your feelings much. You like to work alone because you can think and use your intuition without distraction. When others have suggestions, you listen politely. Their ideas may be helpful, but you still want to be thorough and you're a bit of a perfectionist. You really value quiet and peaceful surroundings. Your home is an ideal place for meditation or intellectual pursuits. Rather than meddle, you give others the space and time they need to work out solutions. It seems to be what you want from them, too. People may not understand you, but they certainly see and appreciate your results.

8 is your IMPRESSION number

Opportunities come easily for you. Life for you seems to be one success after another. You're a good manager. You can lead any sized group and any project you take on will be profitable. Personnel placement and resource management are as natural for you as breathing. People are attracted to you and your ideas. They trust your judgment and know that you have the vision and ability to achieve success. You have all the qualities they would like to see in themselves. With a practical approach to business, you move forward quickly. On the way, you make sure to include the ones who help you. You reach goals through organization and planning. Your basic needs always seem to be taken care of. Your home is comfortable. Personal relationships work out for you. Personable and friendly, you make friendships that are respectful and mutually beneficial. You can make a success of just about anything. Things always work out when you apply yourself. You're always surrounded by a loyal and skilled team of specialists who make your projects successful. Without question, your personal team will follow you in whatever you do.

9 is your IMPRESSION number

Any position of power or authority suits you well. You are a strong, energetic person, ready to take charge of a situation if necessary. As a manager, you direct those under you with compassion, understanding and appreciation. Others follow you and take up your cause because of the air of natural authority you display. People recognize the selfless way you work and hold you in high esteem. They trust your honest and ethical nature. You're confident and give credit to others. That makes you stand out even more. People follow you eagerly because they know they're with the right person. You always seem to know their needs and what to say. They see that you deal with life as necessary and can make the best of almost any situation. You can see all sides of a dispute. As a mediator, you're tops. You're idealistic and have the vision to carry just about any project to completion. You know what you want and will do what is necessary to reach your goals. In the process, you include others in your success. You are a well-rounded individual that can fit in anywhere.

11/2 is your IMPRESSION number

Idealism combined with selfless attitude makes you a good leader. Your idea of a good way of life is very different than anything that already exists. People may not understand your vision but it sounds interesting. You always have a unique plan in the works. You are intuitive, dynamic and insightful. There's almost a mystical quality to you. At times, your ideas show real genius. You see situations from both spiritual and worldly perspectives. When others are at a loss, you often have a solution. People get inspired by the way you view the world. You're very diplomatic and can talk with anyone. Public and private functions seem to be easy for you. You always manage to have a following of people who would like to share in your dreams. You do well in any public situation. Your plans and ideas can make a very real difference in the world.

In addition to the 11, you work from the 2 vibration. That means gentle harmony. It tempers the more high strung 11. You work well with others. Tactful and charming, you bring balance to all relationships. Order is necessary to you and it shows in your life. You can get along with anyone and can see other people's perspectives of things. You are patient and understanding. Aware of others' needs, you give appropriate guidance.

22/4 is your IMPRESSION number

Down to the smallest detail, you seem to see the whole scope of any project. You're a gifted visionary that can turn any idea into a reality. When you're involved, the job gets done. You are very organized and can find a solution to just about any problem. You always seem to know exactly what is needed to get things done. It's almost uncanny the way you place people on a project. No job is too small or too big for you. You can work alone or with others. The way you apply higher values in situations is truly remarkable. Most people don't even understand how you do it. You're intuitive and imaginative. Often your solutions to problems are new and innovative. You can find patterns in what seems like total chaos. Issues that face the world are well within your ability. When there's a special project, people want you on board.

The 4 aspect of 22 is practical. When your higher abilities aren't needed, you are patient and hard-working. One for efficiency, you like a detailed, orderly course of action. You are dependable and people know they can count on you. You don't get emotional with obstacles, you just find a solution. You enjoy hard work and want to be rewarded for it. You can do anything with your hands. You don't complain about what needs to be done and are a very welcome addition to any work force. Once you start work, you stay with it until it's done.

33/6 is your IMPRESSION number
Your specialty seems to be the way you apply spiritual values to help others. You know more about how spiritual and worldly activities tie in than other people do. Most live in the world and spirituality is something they bring into situations. You, on the other hand, live in a spiritual place and use it in the material world as a matter of practice. You separate your own concerns from the needs of others. Then you are available to help when they're ready. If they have a higher purpose, you're there for them. You seem to have the ability to heal. You'd make a good doctor, psychiatrist or healer. Not only do you help others achieve proper health or growth, you show them how to do it for themselves. You can do that on any scale. You could provide these services for entire societies or geographical areas. With such knowledge and abilities, you could be a great spiritual leader.

33 reduced is 6. That's about home and family. You can get along with anyone. You share love and understanding with everyone. You do whatever is needed to make people work well together. Your home and work areas are comfortable and welcoming. You are always ready to help and give sound advice. You fit well in occupations that are for the greater good of the community or country. You're responsible and can be trusted when help is needed. Everyone seems to come to you for advice when they have a problem.

44/8 is your IMPRESSION number
Work environments seem to run smoother when you're involved. When you're in charge, you give credit to those under you. When you're not, you make your superiors look good. Not

only that, but you strive to see that people you don't even work with get treated fairly, as well. People see you as almost saint-like in the way you conduct business. People give you their best because you give them yours. This gives you power and control that few can achieve. You never seem to abuse this power or use it just for personal gain. Even so, you still make personal strides forward quickly. Your focus always seems to be for the best solutions for as many people as possible. You want to make your community a better place for everyone. In the corporate world, you do the same. This means better conditions in the work place. Everyone benefits from your efforts.

44 is also 8. You have a knack for business. With you at the lead, any project can make a profit. Your good business sense propels any project forward. Those under you are successful if they stay with you. Opportunities come easily for you and they usually work out. You seem to do well in personal relationships, too. You are personable and friendly. Everyone gets the same level of respect from you. Employees feel you really care for them. You make friends that are influential and can help you be a success. When you make a friend, it's usually for life.

55/1 is your IMPRESSION number
Ambitious and organized, you make a good leader. You can work with any kind of team or group in any situation. In this, you are the best. You seem to use higher values with logic and intuition. Just about any situation can benefit from your involvement. Those under you work better and conditions improve. Many times, your direction brings unexpected but healthy change. You seem to be the ultimate in freedom of life's many expressions. You live your ideals and think for yourself. You are a versatile mediator, master guide and world traveler all rolled into one. The entire planet is your territory and you cross borders as easily as others go to the corner store. Life for you is exciting and full of potential. You don't intend to miss any of it. You're free in the most literal sense. You can help others enjoy the same freedom as well.

1 is the everyday influence when you need a break from the high power of the 55. People see a pioneer in you. You make plans and carry them out. This can be either with the help of others or you can do it all yourself. You always have fresh ideas where others don't necessarily see solutions. Your style is entirely your own. You don't appear to be one who likes to conform to accepted norms. You initiate new programs or projects and set the direction. It's easy for others to pick up where you leave off. Confidence and courage carry you through any difficulties you may encounter.

66/3 is your IMPRESSION number
Family is very important to you. The world is your home and all in it are your family. To an observer, you don't appear to be concerned with your own needs. Instead, you want to do what's best for others especially when it comes to children and home life. Your approach to life is spiritual and you seem to have your own idea of who, or what, you answer to. Generous and loving, you're there to offer help when it's needed. You're wise enough to not interfere when someone has a problem. If asked for help, though, you freely give whatever advice or assistance you can. With your approach to life, you would be a great spiritual leader. When people have a dispute, you can negotiate for a peaceful solution. You seem to be attracted to things that benefit many people. Wherever you do, others expect the best from you.

The 3 gives more definition to 66. You always have fresh ideas. People see the considerable talent and ability you have. It would seem that you can do just about anything. You often surprise people with some interesting solution to a problem. You're an artist at heart. Even if your profession isn't artistic, you manage to make some part of it that way. You always manage to put your own touch on things. Everyone likes your wit and you are the center of attraction at parties or functions. You have a clean, stylish appearance and can fit in anywhere.

77/5 is your IMPRESSION number
People see you as somewhat of a mystery. You are intelligent, intuitive and innovative. With what appears to be an uncanny connection to the spirit realms, you help people in unconventional ways. You're able to analyze a situation and

quickly identify the key elements. Then you proceed. Your methods are different than most. Although you don't use magic, it sometimes looks like it to others. You do get results where others can't, though. Your solutions to problems often seem almost too simple but they work. You're polite and make friends easily. You can make everyone around you feel special. It's hard to get you into a political discussion. You just don't have an interest in world events unless they are about personal growth. There's a quiet confidence about you that goes unnoticed by many. When you get involved, however, it really shows.

The 5 influence makes it so you don't seem too weird or spacey. Your life is a busy one, full of adventures and excitement. Travel is something you can do for a living, then again for relaxation. Change is fine with you and you obviously can adapt to any new conditions almost immediately. You fit in anywhere and can carry on a conversation with anyone. You are always optimistic and ready to try something new. You look youthful and attractive. With plenty of energy, you take life as it comes. Your movements are quick like your mind.

88/7 is your IMPRESSION number
Where others want to either grow spiritually or build prosperity, you do both. You are a spiritual person and that shows in all parts of your life. You're a good example of discipline and self-control. You change greed into a higher quality and that works for the benefit of everyone. People sometimes wonder how success can come so easily for you. Where they think "money is the root of all evil," you say money results from the application of higher values. You seem to believe that truth and honesty are separate aspects of life that must be combined. It certainly appears to work for you. There are always a number of people who like to be around you. You always treat others more than fairly. You have mastered the business world and may have even made a vast fortune by yourself. Whatever you do, you share your successes with others along the way. You are often involved in projects that are for the good of many people.

The hidden strength of 88 is 7. It puts wisdom and spirituality into your daily dealings. You have an air of nobility but people don't really know what to think of you. You don't seem to need much from them. With sage-like detachment, you research things on your own. You come up with new, often surprising, information or solutions. You like to tap into that special place within yourself. You're confident and somewhat of a perfectionist. Your home is quiet and peaceful. At work, you create a similar space where you can get away from the bustle.

99/9 is your IMPRESSION number
You are a well-rounded person. Traits of all the other numbers can be seen in you. The process of evolution and completion shows through you. You can display completeness and newness at the same time. Your life reflects the idea that the body is the temple of the spirit. It would appear that you believe this. The way you think seems to direct the way you act. You would like to help others understand this, too. You are gifted in music and creative arts. If you don't do art yourself, you may have a genuine appreciation for it. You show compassion, selflessness and a genuine concern for others. You know a lot about health, especially holistic or natural cures. In fact, you seem to know quite a bit about many things. Often people seek your opinion when they need to make a decision. They feel you have the ability to do just about anything you choose to undertake.

The reduced vibration of 9 is a more worldly version of the same energy. You are always ready to take charge. As a leader, you treat those under you with compassion and appreciation. They in turn follow your lead and share your visions as though they were their own. People feel they can trust you. No matter the situation, you always fit in. You see all sides of a situation and treat everyone fairly. People recognize this and respect you for it. You accomplish goals as long as they are within your high ideals. In your success, you always manage to include others.

PART FIVE

Your Higher Purpose

Your ULTIMATE GOAL – Greater Meaning Later On
Destiny # + Expression # or Expression # + Destiny #

Ian Fleming was well-educated but held numerous jobs in his early life with little success. He had applied for entry to the Foreign Office but couldn't pass the exams. He spent a couple years as a sub-editor for Reuters but left that to work as a banker and a stockbroker, both of which didn't work out. Fleming finally got a posting with British Naval Intelligence during WW2. He planned two successful covert operations and started two secret intelligence units. At age 44 he found fame and success as a writer. He drew from his background in intelligence and journalism to write his very popular James Bond novels. Even after he died, two more of his Bond novels were published. Since then, eight more authors have written James Bond stories. The Bond movies are highly popular to this day. Fleming left a legacy we still enjoy.

When Fleming's life took a whole new direction, it was like something kicked in and carried him forward. This section shows an additional, important thing you are to do in this life. It's called your *ultimate goal*. This is in addition to all the other stuff you go through. In fact, it often takes a half a lifetime of experience to even be ready for it. It may sound daunting but in reality, this is when life really gets going for many people. It's no joke when someone says life begins at 50.

The ultimate goal is the most important thing your inner self wants you to accomplish. There's no hard and fast rule for when this comes into your life. It often happens around the time you start to think about retirement. You could be 45 or you could be 70. It may take a while to really get strong. Eventually it becomes your main directing force. If you're unhappy in later years, this might show what you can do to find fulfillment.

To find your ultimate goal, add your destiny and expression numbers together. If both are master numbers, add as master numbers and again as single digits. If just one is a master number, add the single digits only. Here are a few ways it can be added.

Destiny number = 8, expression number = 6
8 + 6 = 14 = 5   ultimate goal = 5

Destiny number = 7, expression number = 4
7 + 4 = 11/2   ultimate goal = 11/2

Destiny number = 4, expression number = 55/1
4 + 1 = 5   ultimate goal = 5

Destiny number = 44/8, expression number = 66/3
44 + 66 = 110 = 2   or   8 + 3 = 11/2   ultimate goal = 11/2

Destiny number = 33/6, expression number = 66/3
33 + 66 = 99/9   6 + 3 = 9   ultimate goal = 99/9

Now, let's look at the ultimate goal for Ian Fleming. His expression number was 3 with a driving force of 84. He was creative. His creativity showed in systematic business or activities. For him, this was his intelligence work during WW2. He saw himself as practical (ambition number 4). Others saw he was good at what he did (impression number 8). His destiny number was 6 with a driving force of 60 and a minor influence of 33/6. His life revolved around support and service.

For his ultimate goal, add his destiny and expression numbers together (6+3=9). 9 brings public exposure to his already creative nature. It also shows he could be a leader in his field. For more insights, add the driving force for both (60+84=144). This shows a resultant driving force of 144. That means practicality, organization and innovation. Fleming's first James Bond novel was an immediate success as they all were. He defined a new kind of leading character for movies, books and TV series. The ultimate goal shows how and why life changed for him.

Early in life, you only need to be aware of what your ultimate goal is. You may even be able to recognize times that prepare you for what is to come. Whether you are years from it or smack in the middle, it helps to know what it is. At the right time, you'll feel the shift.

What Your Ultimate Goal Means

1 is your ULTIMATE GOAL – 9+1, 8+2, 7+3, 6+4, 5+5
This is about life as a free thinker. One who goes into the unknown and starts something new. That can be in the physical, mental, spiritual or emotional planes of existence. Strength and leadership are the qualities you are to learn. You may need to be self-sufficient and operate without any established guidelines or procedures. If you have difficulty working this way, you now have the chance to learn it. All conventions get cast aside for you. You may need to develop new solutions to reach a goal. When you do, things tend to work out better. In a scientific field, this is what you would see in a researcher who lays the groundwork for others in new and exciting directions. Like a pioneer, you can have true freedom of thought and action. When there are no operating rules, make your own. You are goal-oriented and may have to work things out on your own. That's fine because others might slow you down. You like to lead with a hands-on approach. That's more time-effective than to go to all the trouble to document rules and guidelines. Ideally, you'd like others to carry on with the information you provide. If they don't do this, you'll need to help them get started. Your approach should be unique and fresh when you start something. Be confident in your own abilities. It's unlikely you'll feel the need to discuss your ideas or seek approval from others before you start a project or venture.

At times, you may need initiative and assertiveness to get things done. These abilities may be required to help those less capable than you. You may have to defend people, animals or the environment because it's the right thing to do. With courage and confidence, the role of the hero is one you can assume easily. Be humble about it, though.

2 is your ULTIMATE GOAL – 1+1, 9+2, 8+3, 7+4, 6+5
Relationships and partnerships are important now. You have to get along with others and make things work out. The way to accomplish this best is to quietly influence situations or people.

In general, you work best as a support person. This may mean you will teach others how to get along. You may find your place as the real force behind those in charge. When you don't attract much attention, there is personal power you wouldn't otherwise have. Work closely with others to make plans and carry them out. This may or may not be new to you but it's easy to do. Then your greatest reward is found in what you get done. Another area for you to realize your greater purpose is as a mediator. You could have a natural talent for tact, diplomacy and service. If not, you can learn it. There is tremendous strength in this for you. Either way, you must show kindness and charm. Then you'll be able to help opposing parties agree on a solution. All sides of an issue are clear to you. With that, you can identify the options available to those with differences. This helps you negotiate solutions for the best possible benefit of all. Your goal should be to see harmony and balance restored. When in a direct conflict yourself, you'll have to find a solution that is good for everyone. Success in these areas comes from patience and careful planning. The way you can be most effective is to take each step at the right time.

Your love of harmony and communication could lead you into a time rich with self-expression. In addition to other skills, you may have a flair for music, dance or art. This could be quite good if you're not the center of attention. You would be a fine addition to a design team or a musical group. Also, you could be a good supporting actor or part of a dance company. You do best as part of a group where the main purpose is also your personal goal.

3 is your ULTIMATE GOAL – 1+2, 9+3, 8+4, 7+5, 6+6
Self-expression is a strong influence now. Whether you've felt this before or not, you have a need for creative outlet. How you pursue it can vary, depending on your other numbers. It could be in fine art, writing or entertainment. This can be your way to communicate a message to others. You may also find creative expression at home or in business. No matter how you express yourself, it must satisfy that inner need to do something imaginative. Your involvement could be found in the works of

other people. You could deal in art or give support to someone creative. You might do something like custom auto design, specialized furniture or a hobby turned into a venture. Whatever way life goes, you are to learn about self-expression. With your often limitless inner drive, you'll have a constant flow of ideas that need an outlet. You can be upbeat and joyous, even to the point of contagiousness. When you laugh, it's from the heart and others laugh with you. You're entertaining and may have a great command of language. The way you present things is always interesting. No matter what you do, it's destined to be original.

If there are obstacles to your creativity there's something for you to learn from that, too. Also, if you aren't particularly artistic you might find a way to be creative with what you've done in the past. This could come from an occupation or some other activity. There can be new ways to apply your skills that others would overlook. That could propel you forward in your particular field. Your fresh approach can set you off from others. Recognition for what you do gives you a boost. All this could be at home or in any other situation, public or otherwise. Depending on your past experience, fame may very well come to you.

4 is your ULTIMATE GOAL – 2+2, 1+3, 9+4, 8+5, 7+6
There are times when organization and diligence are needed. This is the time for you to apply yourself. There should be plenty of chances to use and hone your practical skills. Things that are useful suit you with this influence. If patience and diligence haven't been strengths for you in the past, you can now learn them. If they have, you can apply them. Hard facts and organization is what works best for you now. The material plane is most likely where you work the most, but it could be on any other level. Whatever you do is easier when you first establish a sound foundation. You have the inner drive to organize things so they move forward to a definite result. The greatest satisfaction will come when you apply yourself. See what's needed and find the best way to do it. Results may be slow but the most practical approach is best for you. If you aren't hard-working, you will probably get the chance to learn that. You can successfully tackle anything you choose. Come up with practical

plans and carry them out in an orderly fashion. Be patient and do the proper preparation before you start a new project. Whatever you have done in life before, it's now easier to see a way to get results. Whatever your chosen profession, you should see an increase in productivity. Everything you do is now more enjoyable with solid plans and well-defined goals.

Your manner should be down to earth, conservative and dignified. When you agree to something, do it. That's a trait you can now develop even more than before. If people seem slow or unproductive to you, organize things so they can be more effective. You may be able to show them how to approach a project to get the best results. A clearly defined plan can give you great satisfaction. Emotional reactions can slow you down so be direct and logical. Your ultimate purpose just may be to produce results. It doesn't matter whether it's for you, for a charitable cause or in an occupation. Pick a good project and follow it through.

5 is your ULTIMATE GOAL – 2+3, 1+4, 9+5, 8+6, 7+7
Transformation and freedom are key elements during this time. Change can make life refreshing and interesting. If your other numbers don't show this, you may have to learn to adapt. If you're a methodical person, variety can provide new ways to apply yourself. There could be many different things of interest for you. When you pick one, it might change on you. You are enterprising and resourceful. You may find it easier to pick up new things. Just about the time a normal person would get comfortable with a profession or activity, you might get bored with it. The best activities for you are those that allow you to grow and change. Life may come at you like a whirlwind but you have the ability to go with it. Because of this, you have the freedom to move in many directions, often at the same time. Travel might be more necessary for you. It can give you a chance to learn about people and develop your social skills to a greater degree. You could even start a new profession that has to do with travel. There could be a need for you to interact with lots of people in different ways. You could pick up new skills and see things differently than before. What may have been

unsettling in the past could now bring greater opportunities. As time passes, you can get more comfortable in new situations.

With this influence, you are very good with your hands. You may also have a sharp mind. You probably have an eye for detail and can make just about anything. This could help you turn out some truly fine works of practical art like furniture or leather goods. Everything about you is quick. This includes your mind, wit, movements and actions. You usually finish projects quickly and come up with shortcuts to get the same or better results in less time. You are unconventional and don't feel tied to accepted methods. Freedom in all its forms is valuable to you. Wherever you find your calling, it should be interesting and full of adventure.

6 is your ULTIMATE GOAL – 3+3, 2+4, 1+5, 9+6, 8+7
Home and family are important to you during this time. You want harmony for everyone. You are most comfortable when people around you have a common goal. This normally means the home or workplace but it can include your community. You could feel a strong sense of responsibility to those in your family or extended family. If this seems like a burden, change your perspective. You may find new friends and associates you wouldn't have thought possible before. Since you understand others, it's easy to see what their needs are. If you don't have good communication skills, this is the time to develop them. There are many chances to help loved ones, friends, associates or strangers. They will probably be drawn to you for help. People trust you to have a genuine concern for their well-being. They will open up to you more than ever before as long as you keep what they say confidential. You may be in a position to help others sort out their problems. Lasting friendships could develop out of this. If it isn't easy to give freely, you now have the opportunity to learn how. The desire to see balance can make you a good advisor. This could be with anyone from young children to heads of state. Family-oriented services or similar occupations may suit you. If politics interests you, be sure you work for the common good.

You are idealistic, fair and devoted. As a caregiver, you are unequaled. This time of your life may bring situations unlike any before. You may have to put others' needs ahead of your own. As well, you may have to let another help you. It's important to learn both sides of this if it happens. Your home is a reflection of an inner desire for harmony. Others feel welcome there and you may offer it to them if they need a place to heal and grow. With the ability to make your home a comfortable living space, you may help others do just that in theirs. Whatever your relationships have been until now, there is a distinct trend toward greater focus on the home.

7 is your ULTIMATE GOAL – 3+4, 2+5, 1+6, 9+7, 8+8
Meditation and introspection are the power tools of your inner self. This period of your life is good for inner guidance. It's time to come up with your own answers rather than rely on those of others. Work things out on your own. It helps to listen to your own guidance for insights and ideas. You can actively access that genius within you for any purpose. Along with this comes an inner peace that is born from your own self-confidence. At this time in life, you most likely aren't drawn to clubs, organizations or scheduled events. You do much better on your own. Go after knowledge and improvement on a personal level. Examine details and analyze data without the need to rely on anyone. To get the best results, you can use intuition with your other abilities. It is not your way to present incomplete ideas for others to mull over. Instead, it's more rewarding for you to know as much as possible before you get others involved. You may tend to be quiet and reserved, especially in a group or gathering. Others could see you as somewhat of a loner but only if they don't understand you. Cultivate a refined manner and you can fit in well with most people.

You need ample time to process information. For this, you have to be removed from the distracting influences of the world around you. You are bright and intelligent but must have time to yourself to work things out. Often, your results seem surprisingly insightful to others. That's just because they don't get to see how much effort and thought you go through. This ultimate goal can be very rewarding as your inner strengths mature. You may develop something new and innovative that others can put to good use. Be sure to allow enough time for your personal growth and development.

8 is your ULTIMATE GOAL – 4+4, 3+5, 2+6, 1+7, 9+8
Success and abundance are rewards you get from efforts properly invested. During this time, you will be in situations that can create material success. It will be necessary for you to be dependable and have good management ability. If this is new for you, you may have to develop it. The result can be a great deal of power and influence. You may have to be shrewd at times but this can be done with diplomacy and tact. You can have good judgment and a practical side to use with discrimination. It may take determination to get what you want at times. With that, you will be able to apply yourself and when you do, the rewards follow. You may work into a management position or act as the CEO of a company. You can not only manage others but help them be successful. In addition, you may teach them how to do it on their own. It's possible that you will mentor someone. The rewards in that are many. To help others manifest success is one of the greater pleasures you can enjoy during this time.

Success is normally associated with business but that's just a part of it. The business sense you develop is useful in many ways. The word 'prosperity' is more to the point than 'success'. Prosperity is a nice home in a good location. It is loving relationships with your spouse and family. It means close friends, good health and well-being. Any area of personal life can bring fulfillment. Outside that, you may work with charities and get far-reaching results for them. Public recognition could come from your efforts. Your focus could be on the home front as the perfect head of your family. Look for that special opportunity if you haven't already identified it. You can expect great rewards to come from all this.

9 is your ULTIMATE GOAL – 4+5, 3+6, 2+7, 1+8, 9+9
Self-benefit isn't as important to your higher purpose as the help you give others. This path may take any form. The actual direction is most likely to be seen in the numbers in your name and birth date. With well-rounded skills, you can do just about anything. You care about people and can help them on many

levels. Honesty and ethics now are more important to you. You can lead or be the strength behind any just cause. Public exposure may also play a part in your life. There could be an opportunity for you in your community instead of business. You can tap into a reservoir of inner strength to get things done. If you want to connect with people, you may do this through art or music. If you aren't particularly creative, you might work in a gallery or museum. You could take a simple idea and make it into a great undertaking. On a smaller scale, you would be ideally placed as a counselor or personal coach. This would probably follow your established direction in life, at least loosely. You can intuitively have the most appropriate information for people who come to you. Your advice and assistance could be exactly what they need. No matter what you do, as long as your focus is with the needs of others you can excel. All you need to have is the appropriate outlet.

Although you may feel a strong inner need to work for the common good, it doesn't mean you have to live like a monk. It just means there is a desire to help your fellow man. Your personal life doesn't need to suffer. The real reward is in what you do to help, anyway. There can be opportunities to help others improve their lives.

11/2 is your ULTIMATE GOAL – 6+5, 7+4, 8+3, 9+2
With a strong sense of idealism, you could work for a cause that benefits all. Your mission is to serve your fellow man. You have an intuitive, maybe even psychic, ability to tap into universal consciousness. With your more spiritual calling, you would make a good intuitive or inspirational teacher. If you haven't been particularly good with words, that should improve. This may be a time of great self-expression for you. There may be a message you want to pass on to others. You could do this as a writer, teacher or public speaker. You could also be an actor or create great works of art. Any of these avenues can be a way for you to reach out to others without them even being aware of it. You can now completely understand a situation and come up with a fresh solution. This time should be full of both activity and challenge for you. Depending on your other influences, you may

do something that benefits large numbers of people. There could be public recognition or fame for you at this time. If so, you should be right at home with it.

2 is the less complex area of partnerships and relationships. This is good when you work with others. Relationships for you can be with one person, small groups, large organizations, governments or the population of a geographical area. This helps you carry out your higher goals. It also gives you a love of harmony and rhythm. It's less important to be in the spotlight than to get results. That doesn't mean to shy away from public attention. It just gives you a different perspective. At times when you don't need the higher energy, you can enjoy more harmony and sensitivity. Read about the 2 ultimate goal to get a better idea of what it can mean for you.

22/4 is your ULTIMATE GOAL – 11+11
Idealism combines with inspired vision to see great possibilities. Practicality helps you make them a reality. You can now do anything you put your mind to. No matter what you have done in the past, you are better equipped than ever. Before you start anything, you see what's needed in detail. That way you know what has to happen long before you commit to it. A good plan makes it easy for you to get things done. Your plans can be both practical and complete. To get the best results, you can apply higher values to worldly situations. This is good for anything from vacation plans to large technical projects. You could be involved with activities that help many people, such as agricultural plans or programs for the needy. Projects like these take money. Instead of a direct involvement in them, you may look to build a vast empire of wealth that can in turn be used to promote such ventures. You may work up plans that others will carry out in the future. On either a personal or global scale, you are to build something that can help others for years to come.

Your higher purpose is supported by the practical value of 4. This underlying number is always there for you. It provides the ability to step forth and get things done. With this in your tool box, you're always busy with some kind of project. You first build a good foundation then apply yourself. Work is your friend and you will tackle any task. You like practical plans and have the patience to prepare properly. Results follow in accord with the effort you spend. Whatever you do, you can apply yourself with skill and dedication. Read about the 4 ultimate goal so you can further understand its influence.

33/6 is your ULTIMATE GOAL – 11+22
It's now easier for you to understand people. You may be surprised at the clarity you have in this. With that and a large measure of compassion, you can find a good way to help them. This gives you a chance to help others, then teach them what they need to stay in balance. This way you can heal others on a deeper level. Patient and wise, you have what it takes to be a great healer, teacher or spiritual leader. Chances are you are highly enlightened and self-realized. If not, you may work on just that. If it wasn't the case before, you now are able to understand the issues others have. Your focus is more on higher learning than physical needs. You can see how inner issues relate to people's physical problems. With a more spiritual approach, you could help others realize their greatest potential. Another area for you may be in the field of health care, especially with natural cures and herbs. A quality that should help with that is the ability to identify the inner causes of physical problems. Since all levels of being are spiritual, you can show others how to change what they do on one level to get a result on another. The most fulfilling thing for you is to help others with their issues and problems.

The additional influence of the 6 focuses more on home and family. It means a lot to you to see harmony in the lives of those close to you. Friendships you now make can last a lifetime. People sense your genuine concern and trust you with their inner secrets. You may need to put others' needs ahead of your own. You could feel drawn to family-oriented services or occupations. Familiarize yourself with the definition of the 6 ultimate goal. With its calming influence, you can really make a difference in people's lives.

44/8 is your ULTIMATE GOAL – 11+33, 22+22
With great power and vision, you can change the way people go about their lives. You are able to show them there is no separation of physical and higher levels of being. All you've learned on a spiritual level can be used for the material benefit of others. You could start programs to help people provide for their own basic needs. As well, you might help them with the supplies or education to be self-sufficient. This does more than merely give them what they need physically. It helps them on a deeper, more lasting level. With your help, they can change their basic approach to life. Another way you could help is to provide spiritual wealth for people on a worldly level. You could educate people to properly use the resources of the planet. Ideally, this is done with projects that preserve the natural condition of the planet. They could then learn how the Earth nurtures us. That perspective provides balance on all levels. In turn, it benefits all of mankind. Everyone likes to see material success. Material wealth for its own sake is limiting and destructive, though. For you, it's more important to make a lasting and positive change that helps everyone.

As a complimentary influence, 8 is there for you. You can be practical, innovative, shrewd or diplomatic if needed. This could make you a manager or CEO of a corporation. Monetary success is just part of the overall picture, though. Prosperity is more to the point for you. That can be seen in your home, relationships and personal well-being. You may be active in just about any activity that provides a reward. Know the meaning of the 8 ultimate goal. It can really help with your ultimate purpose. Look for opportunities. When one appears, take it.

55/1 is your ULTIMATE GOAL – 11+44, 22+33
With a keen sense of intuition, your "hunches" can pay off when there isn't enough information to make a calculated decision. You are a knowledgeable and capable leader. You can lead anyone and what the project is doesn't matter. What's important is how you do it. You have a limitless supply of energy and can focus it on anything. People feel your confidence and follow you without question. The whole planet is your domain. Distance and borders don't affect you. At times, you may need to change your function to reach a goal. That's easy for you. You need

total freedom whether it's mental, physical, emotional or spiritual. You want others to have it, too. You may have a strong interest in metaphysics or spirituality. The projects you take on reflect your spiritual approach. As the master of many skills, you can apply them all to bring transformation on a grand scale. Since change is in your blood, you can show others how to work with it, too. Public attention doesn't excite you other than for the boost it gives your projects.

The power behind you is 1, the true leader and pioneer. It powers the higher, more spiritual energy. This gives you the way to carry out your ultimate purpose. You prefer to work by yourself rather than let others slow you down. At times when others are involved, you lead by example since it is more time-effective. You just don't like to waste time with official rules and guidelines. The way you pursue a goal is always unique and fresh. The 1 helps with courage and assertiveness when you need to get something done. You are confident so the role of the hero is one you can assume easily. Familiarize yourself with the 1 ultimate goal to further understand its influence.

66/3 is your ULTIMATE GOAL – 11+55, 22+44, 33+33
This is a time for you to work for the benefit of many. You're a caring and domestic person. As such, you do well in situations that relate to family life and children. The home is where you are most comfortable. You want it to be the perfect place. The concept of home can include the community, country or planet. You may be called on to keep peace or settle disputes. You get a good measure of fulfillment to work for the benefit of children and families. The key is harmony and you may find creative ways to provide it for others. When there is a dispute, you can find solutions that are good for everyone. Your spiritual approach to life helps you work things out where others wouldn't see any solution. You see the real reasons behind disagreements and work around those issues. With a more universal purpose, you could be drawn into international issues and work to make peace on a global level. With your high ideals, the universe is your home and you answer to the highest

order. You could find your place as a spiritual leader and touch the lives of millions.

The reduced value of 3 means originality and self-expression. You can be creative in the way you help others. You could choose to share ideas through works of art. You are good with words and can show your thoughts to others in clear, pleasant images. Friendly and entertaining, you draw others into your life to enjoy your dreams. However you use your creativity, it will be fueled by a continuous flow of original ideas. You can make a real difference for people either locally or on a global scale. Since the 3 ultimate goal is present also, be sure to read about it for the greatest advantage.

77/5 is your ULTIMATE GOAL – 11+66, 22+55, 33+44
There are those who have a strong connection to the spirit realms. It's like that for you, especially now. The concerns of the physical world may only get enough attention to get you by. Fairly advanced spiritually, you tend to go within for exploration and growth. You prefer to find your own way to enlightenment rather than depend on others to show the way. It's easy for you to work on higher planes of existence. You can go there to get information to be applied in the physical world. Your real purpose may be along the lines of an applied mystic or shaman. As such, you could use spiritual powers to affect real change in the world. Or, you could easily be a prophet or sage. With loving detachment, you let others experience life in their own way. You understand people in ways that few even suspect possible. You may write books and give classes to help others grow. You could easily become a remote healer or psychic. You may use the tools at your disposal to help people with their issues. You are intelligent, inventive and insightful. One way or another, you are to bring new information into the physical plane for the betterment of all.

5 gives you additional boost and support. It's more immersed in the physical world and brings balance to your life. This makes it easier to interact with others. It also helps make your message interesting and entertaining. You can talk to any person or group because you intuitively pick up their thought patterns. You then deliver information in a way they can understand. The 5 may

also bring a degree of travel into your life. Your higher purpose can be exciting on many levels. Know what the 5 ultimate goal means since it applies to you as well.

88/7 is your ULTIMATE GOAL – 11+77, 22+66, 33+55, 44+44
Prosperity can be found in any area of life. You're to find the balance between it and spirituality. It's not only a monetary reward but the satisfaction of a job well done. You could find an activity or profession that lets you express your inner self. It can also be found in the people you work with and much, much more. You may amass a great deal of wealth in your chosen field. You know success is best made with the use of spiritual principles. There could be many chances to learn what to do with abundance once it's yours. You must master all aspects of prosperity and what it means to have it. The tools of success are yours to use wisely. Whether you use them just for self-gain or for the betterment of all will make a difference. You can make temptation or desire a positive force. Fulfillment can be found in family, friends, natural beauty, artistry, craftsmanship or technology. The list is endless. Although business is the most obvious way to have it in your life, it could be in a whole different area. Keep your attention on the abundance in your life and what it can mean.

The reduced value of 7 is always there to help you. This means wisdom and guidance. You may need to go inward for guidance to carry out your mission. You can come up with your own answers rather than rely on others. This can bring inner peace and confidence to apply in your daily life. You are bright and intelligent and can work things out on your own. Be sure to read the definition of the 7 ultimate goal. With the power of that to back your play, you can combine the spiritual and physical to realize your greatest potential.

99/9 is your ULTIMATE GOAL – 11+88, 22+77, 33+66, 44+55
This is the end of a full cycle and the gateway into the next. You carry forward what you have learned. Any or all of that may be useful in this life. The things you have left undone are available for you to finish. You may have a chance to use spiritual

methods and principles. You know the body is the temple of the spirit. You understand how the world works and see patterns where others don't. Gifted in arts or music, you can be creative in anything you do. There are no limits to your abilities. You can literally do anything you set your mind to. With a genuine concern for others, you can work in any capacity. You could be a spiritualist or a farm laborer. As long as you can help others, you are in your proper place. The other numbers in your numerology should give information to the way your ultimate purpose might be expressed. 99 is a spiritual amplification of the other influences. It merges all levels of being into physical expression.

The reduced value of 9 is basically the same on a more worldly level. You are idealistic and honest. You can make a simple idea into a great accomplishment. As a leader, you could show others how to do projects that can help many people. Personable and full of energy, you can be the strength behind any just cause. On a smaller scale, you could be a good counselor or personal coach. When people come to you for guidance, you have exactly what they need. Focus is on what is best for others and you'll excel. You may find purpose in opportunities that come your way. Read about the 9 ultimate goal for further insights.

PART SIX

More in Your Life

Your SIGNATURE NAME – The Everyday You

Years ago, I had a car that was lots of trouble. Something always needed attention. I checked the VIN number with numerology. It didn't indicate problems. That was good since the only way to change a VIN is to get rid of the car. The license number was a different story, though. It totaled to a number that can mean difficulty for me. I turned in the old plates for new ones. When they arrived, the numerical total was different. With the new plates installed, the car never gave any trouble again. A new license number changed the nature of the car.

The name on your birth certificate is like a VIN number. It was given to you at birth and stays the same all through life. The name you use every day is your signature name. It's like the license number on your car. Change it and its influence changes.

A name change adds an additional influence. You can take another name by marriage or other legal change of name. Actors, artists and writers often take on a stage or pen name. Nicknames are used by friends, relatives or close associates. Even an alias has its own influence. All have an effect but the name you were born with is always the strongest influence.

The easiest name change is your signature. It becomes the "you" that meets the world and represents the personal way you interact with others. You put it on business cards and letters. It's how you sign checks, letters and contracts. It can be personal or professional. You may choose to abbreviate your middle name with an initial. Also you may go by a less formal version of your first name, like Joe instead of Joseph or Becky in place of Rebecca. Regardless of how you sign your name, it affects your life. You can use numerology to choose a signature that's best for your needs.

Here's an example of a full name and different ways to vary the signature.

Samuel Langhorne Clemens
Samuel L. Clemens
Samuel Clemens
Sam Clemens
Sam L. Clemens
S. Langhorne Clemens
S. L. Clemens
S. Clemens

Notice how different each one is. Some sound more formal than others. Each could very easily be used. Our example, of course, chose the pen name "Mark Twain" to work under for his writing but surely used one or more of the others in his life.

Now check the numerology. For these we'll look at just the expression numbers. A thorough analysis would need to include all the influences but this is just a quick look. This list includes his pen name.

Samuel Langhorne Clemens = 11/2
Samuel L. Clemens = 1
Samuel Clemens = 7
Sam Clemens = 5
Sam L. Clemens = 8
S. Langhorne Clemens = 4
S. L. Clemens = 3
S. Clemens = 9
Mark Twain = 11/2

Each name has its own influence. Clemens was probably known as 'Sam Clemens' much of the time. That name means travel, adventure and variety. In his early life he was a printer, writer, editor, steamboat pilot, prospector, traveler and reporter. Around 1865 he took the pen name 'Mark Twain' and became famous as a writer and story teller.

A look at Clemens' birth name, his most likely common name and his pen name shows why.

Samuel Langhorne Clemens	=92=11/2 expression
Sam Clemens	=32=5 expression
Mark Twain	=38=11/2 expression

His birth and pen names show creativity, communication, insight and fame. As Sam Clemens, he traveled a lot and knew variety and excitement. Although he wrote early in life, success came after he chose his pen name. The driving force is important in this instance. For 'Mark Twain' it's 'business' and 'creativity'. That combination was new to him with his pen name.

His destiny number was 22/4. That shows the practical influence to be successful. He certainly had success in his day and his writings are still well known and enjoyed by many.

A signature name can add an influence that may not be there in existing numbers. In the case of 'Mark Twain', the needed influence was provided by the driving force. More often, the expression brings the change.

Louise Snyfeld once told me that Cecil B. DeMille was not successful at first. His career really took off after she advised him to use his middle initial in his signature name. Here's why.

Cecil Blount DeMille =77/5
Cecil DeMille =56=11/2
Cecil B. DeMille =58=4

The 77 in his birth name shows creative genius, inventiveness and insight. Reduced to 5 it's freedom, change and adventure. His destiny number was 11/2. That shows a creative idealist full of artistic ability, romanticism, fame and inspiration. As a 2, it meant he worked well with others. 'Cecil DeMille' was 11/2 like his destiny. An 11 may not be able to put his ideas into action. He needed help to get things done. The "B" made his signature name total to 4. That added practicality, application and organization to the way he worked. The driving force was business and adaptability. It was exactly what he needed.

Gandhi was born Mohandas Karamchand Gandhi. 'Mahatma' was a name given to him by a writer named Tagore. He never officially took the name but was often called that. In the West, many think that was his real name. Earlier in this book we saw that his destiny number was 99/9. That means divine wholeness, enlightenment and completion.

Mohandas Karamchand Gandhi =102=3 expression
Mahatma Gandhi = 55/1 expression

Gandhi's birth name is 3. That shows freedom, change and travel. The driving force is 102 which means a diplomatic pioneer. In short, that was his whole life. He was schooled as a lawyer in London. His name (3) and destiny (99) show innovation on higher levels. He helped bring political and social change to South Africa and India. 'Mahatma Gandhi' is 55/1 which means master guide, natural leader and visionary. There were many devout followers of his civil, political and spiritual movements. 99 and 55 together show the spiritual pioneer he was in later years.

A signature name can help with your goals and mission in life. These examples are done with just the expression and destiny numbers. You should consider all the influences in your chart when you do this, though. Ambition numbers and impression numbers make a difference.

Pen names, aliases, nicknames and other secondary names all have an influence. You may use more than one. A writer will have a birth name, a signature name and possibly several pen names for different types of writing. The writer Donald Westlake wrote under 16 pen names plus his own. I knew an investor who had a legal name change for use just outside the country. A name is how you interact with the world so don't be in a hurry. The more carefully you choose a signature name, the better it will meet your needs.

BRANDS, ADDRESSES and OTHER NUMBERS

On final approach, I held the Cessna steady at 75 knots. A tumbleweed twirled on the runway ahead. I crossed the threshold, reduced power and started to slow for touchdown. Suddenly, the plane violently twisted to the left, almost completely sideways to the runway. Before I could react, the plane abruptly pointed down the runway again, right wing low. I leveled the wings and stayed lined up. The plane dropped onto the runway with a thump. It wasn't my best landing but the plane was down, undamaged. I had flown through a dust devil. One of those could flip a plane on its back on the runway and it almost happened to me.

The airport was familiar, I had many hours in that airplane and my skills were sharp. An unexpected force had changed the outcome. The warning sign was the tumbleweed spinning on the runway but I didn't recognize it. Had I known what it meant, I would have aborted my approach and landed on a different runway.

There are significant influences other than those in your name and birth date. They can change your experience in life. All you have to know is where to look and what they mean.

Is your home comfortable? Does it support the lifestyle you want? How about your business or place of work? You spend a lot of time there. It has a bearing on how you feel and the results you get. In addition to your work address, the name of the company affects your success.

A resume with keywords and strengths from your chart shows what you can do for an employer. It can be tailored to show the traits they should see in you.

Vehicles and brand-name items can affect you. Why is one car a good one for you and another just the opposite. Appliances or other major purchases can give great service or not, too. You can carry this as far as you want but the brand of a pen or bar of soap generally isn't that important. Numerology is a good tool, just don't get carried away.

Addresses

A home or business address directly affects you. Numerology shows you how it can.

There are two important influences in an address. One is the street number. Like a personality, it's a quick look at how a location feels and the activities it supports. The other is the complete address with everything spelled out plus the street number and zip code. This tells the overall influence and what activities are best carried out.

Written out fully, an address is like your birth name. It gives the strongest influence. When you abbreviate things like the state, St., Dr., Ave. or others, it changes the totals much like your signature name does. This allows you to pick the best way to write it for business cards, stationery, return addresses, etc. The full address is still the strongest influence, though.

Calculate the address like a name. Numbers have no ambition or impression but do add to the expression. Here's how it looks.

240 Viola Drive, Aromas, California 95004

```
          16            14          8               26
          96 1          9 5      1  6  1         1  9 6    91
240(=6)  VIOLA(=23=5)  DRIVE(=31=4)  AROMAS(=22/4)  CALIFORNIA(=52=7)  95004(=18=9)
          4  3          4 9 4        9  4  1       3  36  95
           7             17           14              26
```

To make it a size we can see, here are just the calculations from the address:

```
   16 + 14 +  8  + 26          =64=10=1  AMB
6 + 23 + 31 + 22 + 52 + 18     =152=8    EXP
    7 + 17 + 14 + 26           =64=10=1  IMP
```

The street number is the most important single aspect. This one is 240 which reduces to 6. It would feel comfortable and nurturing. Since there is no driving force, use the whole number (240) for more insight. That would show high potential in practical relationships.

The 8 expression (total of everything including numbers) shows that it's a good address for business or networking. The driving force is 152. That means it is a place to build relationships that offer many new ideas. If this were a residence, it would be a good home office. Clients would be comfortable there. The 1 ambition and 64 driving force indicates that it would be easy to follow schedules and do innovative work. With the same influence for the impression number, visitors would see it as a place for fresh ideas and practical results.

Overall, this address is great for business. It's easy to work things out. This place could be used for meetings of all kinds. It's great for an architect, interior decorator, family lawyer, psychiatrist or consultant.

To some degree, variations of the address can help to change the influence. The mailing address you choose is much like a signature name. It adds an additional influence.

Here it is with "Drive" and "California" abbreviated.

```
           16                       8            1
           96  1                1   6  1         1
240 (=6)  V I O LA (=23=5)  D R (=13=4)  A R O MA S (=22/4)  C A (=4) 95004 (=18=9)
           4   3                4 9         9   4  1         3
           7                    13            14            3
```

Again, just the calculations:

```
     16 + -- +  8 + 1           =25=7     AMB
6 + 23 + 13 + 22 + 4 + 18       =86=14=5  EXP
     7 + 13 + 14 + 3            =37=10=1  IMP
```

Now the expression is 5 with a driving force of 86. That would emphasize versatility in a supporting business. The 7 ambition is good for research or occult. A psychic or detective would do very well there. As a home, it would be good for meditation, shamanic journeying or remote viewing. The impression is still for fresh ideas but with more research and creativity behind them.

If you write out Drive and abbreviate CA, the influences would change slightly.

```
          16            14             8            1
          96  1         9   5      1   6   1        1
240 (=6)  V I O LA(=23=5)  D R I V E(=31=4)  A R O MA S(=22/4)  C A (=4) 95004 (=18=9)
          4   3         4 9  4      9   4   1        3
          7             17            14            3
```

The calculations:

```
     16 + 14 +  8 + 1            =39=12=3  AMB
6 + 23 + 31 + 22 + 4 + 18        =104=5    EXP
     7 + 17 + 14 + 3             =41=5     IMP
```

Now it means variety and adventure. The driving force is 104 for plans and new ideas. The ambition is 3. That shows more creativity for the occupants. The impression is 5. Visitors or clients would expect something more exciting. A vacation planner or nature photographer would do well there.

Each city or town has a particular influence by itself. 'Aromas' is a 22/4. It's where you get things done with vision and inspiration. It also helps with practicality and organization. 'Aromas, California' is an 11/2 for creativity and idealism. The 2 means Aromas is a good place to work with others. With the zip code it's still 11/2.

If you want to change the location of your home or business, first see what's out there. Often, there's something available that's better than you would have imagined. If what's available won't work, keep looking. Properties come on the market all the time. The right one will be there at exactly the right time.

Business Names/Names in Business

I saw a good adventure movie that had been out for a while. It hadn't been very successful in the box office. I almost didn't watch it because the name sounded boring. The write-up did sound interesting so I gave it a try anyway. It was fun to watch and I enjoyed it a lot. When I told a friend about it, he said he passed it up because from the name, he didn't think he'd like it. Both of us thought the same thing. There had to be something in the numerology.

The expression number of the movie name meant benevolence, organization, a practical leader. That's great for a documentary but not for an adventure film. I checked two other movies of the same type that were very successful. Both names meant initiative, daring and a courageous leader. Clearly the movie's success was affected by the name. A better name may have helped it at the box office. It pays to check these things in advance.

Any business or organization is affected by names just like you are. The company name, an advertising slogan or the name of a motion picture directly affects success. There are three considerations in a good name. The name should sound good. It should also make linguistic sense. Mainly, a name should support the purpose of the venture. To do that, you must understand the subtle influences. Numerology is the way to see what those influences are and how they affect business.

With a business name, use the exact legal name the way it is on the original papers when the business was formed. That's the same as a birth certificate is for a person. For a new business use the name as it will be. It makes a difference if "Incorporated" is written as "Inc." or "Limited Liability Company" is "LLC".

Joe and Larry want to start a mining company. They choose the name Gold Dust, Inc.

```
   6              3              9          =18=9 AMB
   6              3              9
 G O L D (=20=2)  D U S T (=10=1)  I N C (=17=8)   =47=11/2 EXP
 7  3 4         4  1 2          5 3
   14             7              8          =29=11/2 IMP
```

The expression is 11/2. 11 shows that the business would be idealistic and work for the benefit of everyone involved. The 2 means good working relationships. That affects partners and anyone they deal with. The 9 ambition is honesty, ethics and completion. That's what the partners would want to live up to.

The impression is also 11/2 so others would see the business exactly as it is.

The individual words are minor influences. "Gold" has a 2 expression for partnering, "Dust" is a 1 for pioneering and "Inc." is an 8 for prosperity. This is great for a mining partnership.

Suppose the primary purpose of the business was mining research. Joe and Larry would then want a different name. They could combine their names and have "JoeLarr Findings, Inc."

```
    12              18             9          =39=3 AMB
  6 5  1          9  9           9
 J O E L A R R (=34=7)  F I N D I N G S (=46=1)  I N C (=17=8)   =97=7 EXP
 1   3  9 9       6  5 4 5 7 1    5 3
    14              7              8          =37=10=1 IMP
```

The 7 expression is good for research. The 3 ambition means they could be creative in their approach to the work and the 4 impression would show them practical and hard working. A well-chosen name can help make a venture successful.

Keywords

There are times when you will write about yourself. At those times, you want the words to clearly represent you. Numerology can help you do this is with the use of keywords. The best places to find them are in your expression and ambition numbers. It's easy, just look up the definitions for those numbers and read the keywords listed there. Then use the appropriate ones in your text. Synonyms can be substituted for the listed keywords, too.

A classic place to use keywords is in a resume. Employers want to know what you can do for them. Your work history shows what you did for other companies. With numerology, your resume can show you at your best.

Here's how you do it. For this example, the expression number is 4 and the impression number is 9. The keywords for the expression are "details," "orderly," "organization," "results," "responsible," "economical," "application," "practical," "efficient," and "logical." The impression keywords are "balance," "completion," "trust," "strength," "leadership," and "service."

It doesn't hurt to say that you were the one who did the work. Be proud to claim credit as long as you don't use the word "I" too much.

Without the keywords:

1999-2005 John Duncan Foundry – shop foreman
*   Duties: I scheduled production, ordered materials and placed employees as needed. During this period, the shop was more productive. We met manufacturing demands better than ever before. Overhead was lower and profits were up 7% per man hour over the entire period.*

With the keywords in bold print:

1999-2005 John Duncan Foundry – shop foreman
*Duties: I was hired to **balance** production schedules with materials availability. It was my **responsibility** to place **trustworthy** personnel in key positions and **organize** shop procedures. With my **leadership** the company enjoyed greater **efficiency** in manufacturing and a 7% increase in profits per man hour for the entire period.*

Keywords should show your ability to meet the company's needs. In a longer resume, you'd probably use more as long as they sound appropriate. You probably wouldn't want to repeat them a lot, though.

This example is how to use numerology. On a different note, know your market. These days, some employers choose to eliminate applicants that use certain buzz words. Be sure to know what those might be for your profession so you don't work against yourself.

Submit your resume on a 1 day. As a reminder, the daily influence is the sum of all the numbers in the date. The date 12/20/2012 was a 1 day (1+2+2+0+2+0+1+2=10=1). When you get accepted, try to start work on a 1 day. If you can't, don't stress over it. Use numerology to your advantage when you can. It gives you an edge.

Vehicles

Everyone who drives has had a memorable car. It may have been good or it could have been a bad one. Each car has a unique "personality" and Numerology can show what that is.

164

The year, make and model show the overall influence. Use the manufacturer's exact model designation. "2003 Dodge Grand Caravan Sport AWD" is 134=8. Such a vehicle should be a good investment, practical, user-friendly and reliable. My wife and I have one. That certainly is the case. There are times when the AWD pulled us out of tough places.

Each car has a unique Vehicle Identification Number or VIN. This shows how it will be for maintenance and operation. In some ways, it's the most important single influence. The VIN number is a long series of letters and digits assigned when it was made. The car above totals to 79=7. 7 means it's designed well and will work without problems. 79 means dependable and well-thought out. It's all of that.

License plates are like a signature name. Don't let a license number keep you from buying a good vehicle. You can get new plates. The license number for our Caravan totals to 27=9. 9 would mean it has an additional influence for service and trustworthiness. The driving force is 27 for perfection of service. It lives up to that, too.

It's a good idea to total all three influences, too. Here's how the Caravan works out.

2003 Dodge Grand Caravan Sport AWD =134=**8**
VIN =79=16=**7**
License Number =27=**9**
134+79+27=**240**=**6**

Overall, this vehicle should be a good investment (8) that is designed well (7) and provides good service (9). It should work for our needs (6 for support and service) and be practical and easy to drive (4 for practicality and 2 for easy to get along with). This car is so useful it will be with us for a long time.

What is your vehicle? See how it lives up to the numbers.

Focus on items that really matter. Don't worry about the rest. If there is something you need that's costly or important, calculate the numbers. Law enforcement personnel would do well to check the numbers on a firearm since lives could depend on it. Most likely, things without serial numbers won't affect you much. At least, all items of the same brand and model will work much the same as all others. It's good practice to calculate things in your life that have serial numbers and model designations to see how they have performed for you.

WHAT'S NEXT?

Master Numerology explains the main influences in your name and birthday. Now you know what you were born to do in life. You also know the best way to go about it. In addition to that, you can plan on your higher purpose. This book has definitions of the numbers, both basic and specific to their use. One section shows you ways to use these numbers in your business and other parts of your life. There are countless applications for the techniques shown in this book. You only need to use your imagination. Now you should be ready to move forward with greater confidence.

If you apply what's in this book, your life experience can be richer and more productive. When you understand your special strengths and how to use them, everything can be done with purpose and planning. In short, you have an edge available only with numerology. In this, you really do have the operator's handbook for life.

GLOSSARY OF TERMS

When you read a new book on numerology, questions may come up. "What does he mean by, 'destiny number'? It looks like he's talking about the 'expression number'. Then again, it might be the 'life path' he's referring to. Or, maybe it's... Why isn't there a list of terms so I can tell what he *does* mean?"

Sound familiar? There are different schools of thought with numerology. Depending on which one you learned, your terms may be very different than someone else's. No one seems to speak the same language. Often, half the battle with a new book on the subject is to figure out what the writer is talking about. Astrologers have it easy. Say 'Gemini' or 'Pluto' and everyone knows what that is. In numerology, the only term everyone seems to agree on is how to spell 'numerology'.

Here's my glossary of terms so you will know what I mean. You can look up my term to see what it is. You should also be able to look up your term and know what I call it. To the best of my ability, I have cross-referenced everything in this glossary to equivalent terms used by others. The terms used in this book are in bold print so you can easily identify them.

Alias: See *signature name*.

Ambition Number: The total of the numerical values of the vowels in your birth name. Called *heart's desire*, *motivation number* or *soul urge* by some.

Assumed Name: See *signature name*.

Birth Date: The date you were born. This is always written month/day/year, even in parts of the world where the date is written differently.

Birth Year: The year you were born. It's normally reduced to a single digit. There are several ways to calculate do this to see if a **master number** is present. For more on the calculations see the section about **destiny number**.
Cardinal Number: Any of the single-digit numbers 1 through 9.

Challenge: The non-beneficial way any characteristic of a number can be expressed. This can happen when a person fails to take advantage of the **opportunity**. This is very different than a *life challenge*.

Common Name: The less formal name used with friends or associates. This may or may not be the same as your *signature name*.

Concord: See *sign*.

Core Numbers: The most important numbers in a numerology chart. They consist of the **destiny number, ambition number, impression number, expression number** and **ultimate goal**.

Current Name: See *signature name*.

Daily Influence: The specific numerical influence of each day found by adding the month, day and year together.

Day of Birth: The day of the month you were born.

Destiny Number: The reduced total of your birth date. There are several ways to calculate this and all must be done to look for **master numbers**. This may be called *life path* or *life number* by some.

Driving Force: The total of a multi-digit number before it is reduced. This is taken into consideration for more understanding of an influence. This can also be called the *undercurrent* or *supporting value*.

Expression Number: The sum of the numerical values of all the letters in your full name at birth. Some call this the *destiny number* (this should not be confused with the total of your birth date which is what I learned to call the **destiny number**).

Heart's Desire: See **ambition number**.

Heart Self: See **impression number**.

Impression Number: The total of the numerical values of the consonants in your full birth name. Some call this the *personality number*, *quiescent self* or *heart self*.

Life Path number: See **destiny number**.

Life Number: See **destiny number**.

Married Name: See **signature name**.

Master Numbers: The numbers 11, 22, 33, 44, 55, 66, 77, 88 and 99.

Maturity number: See **ultimate goal**.

Motivation Number: See **ambition number**.

Nickname: See **signature name**.

Numerology: The science of the influence of numbers and how they affect your life.

Pen Name: See **signature name**.

Personality Number: See **impression number**.

Prosperity Number: The number that provides an additional influence of prosperity for each of the three **signs**.

Professional Name: See **signature name**.

Pseudonym: See *signature name*.

Quiescent Self: See *impression number*.

Short Name: See *signature name*.

Sign: One of three basic modes of life experience. Also known as a *concord*.

Signature Name: The name you use in business or for daily use. This can be a married name, assumed name, stage name, nickname, alias, pseudonym, pen name, common name or any other name used in addition to, or in place of, your birth name.

Single-Digit Number: Any of the numbers 1 through 9. Also called *cardinal number*.

Soul Urge: See *ambition number*.

Spiritual Birthday: Days when the *daily influence* is the same as your *destiny number*.

Stage Name: See *signature name*.

Supporting Value: See *driving force*.

Ultimate Goal: The reduced total of your *destiny number* and *expression number*. Called *maturity number* by some.

Undercurrent: See *driving force*.

World Year: The calendar year from January 1st through December 31st. Also referred to as the *current year* or *universal year*.

<u>NOTES</u>

www.ingramcontent.com/pod-product-compliance
Lightning Source LLC
LaVergne TN
LVHW051632080426
835511LV00016B/2306